a Complementary book for the
arcadia Free Public Library
On memory of my wife Josephine,

Erv Walth

Erwin G. Walth
121 14th St NE, Suite 801
Rochester, MN 55906
(507) 285-0297

HORSE SENSE
FOR STABLE MINDS

Humorous grains of thought
to sustain you through life

ERWIN G. WALTH

Sage
Creek
Press

Traverse City, Michigan

Published by SAGE CREEK PRESS
121 E. Front Street, 4th Floor
Traverse City, Michigan 49684

Publisher's Cataloging-in-Publication Data
Walth, Erwin G.
   Horse sense for stable minds: humorous grains of thought to sustain you
   through life / Erwin G. Walth. -- Traverse City, Mich.: Sage Creek Press, 1999.
      p.   cm.
   ISBN 1-890394-25-4
   1. Epigrams, American. 2. American wit and humor. I. Title.
PN6281.W35   1999   98-60602
818.5402   dc—21   CIP

PROJECT COORDINATION BY JENKINS GROUP, INC.

03 02 01 00 ❖ 5 4 3 2 1

Printed in the United States of America

*To Josephine, my loyal and loving wife for forty-eight years.
Even after her death on November 22, 1997, she is my
motivation to live. I'm truly grateful for the wonderful years
we spent together.*

CONTENTS

Preface   ix

Acknowledgments   xi

Introduction   xiii

ABOUT AND BY THE AUTHOR   1
   On the Lighter Side   2
   A Blizzard As Found Only During The 1930's
   In The Western Dakotas   10
   Eager To Earn Some Spending Money
   For The Coming Years   12
   Memories Of A Seven-Year Drought And
   Seven Years Of Crop Failure In South
   Dakota During The 1930's   15

COLLECTIONS & OBSERVATIONS   19

AGING   121

BITS OF WISDOM   131

FAITH & RELIGION   149

FRIENDSHIP, LOVE & MARRIAGE   163

PERSONAL GROWTH & VIRTUE   185

GOVERNMENT & POLITICS   197

THOUGHTS WHILE SHAVING   211

WORK   233

QUESTIONS   247

DEFINITIONS   259

THE OUTHOUSE   275
Contributions From Friends

ORDER INFORMATION   283

PREFACE

Humor Words of Wisdom
Stories Humility
Quotes Personal Growth
Anecdotes Virtues
Groaners Hope
One-Liners Serious Thoughts

FROM HUMBLE BEGINNINGS ON A SOUTH DAKOTA FARM through a lifetime as a successful businessman, Erwin G. Walth has extolled and exemplified the traits of hard work, self-reliance, common sense (he calls it horse sense), honesty, faith, and especially humor.

A witty man himself, he began collecting quips and jokes at an early age. As he accumulated experience over the years, he began to record his own reflections and observations on human traits, foibles, and triumphs. Now he has collected his favorite jokes, anecdotes, and bits of wisdom in a book that is as inspiring as it is funny, as warm as it is bright.

"The primary message I wish to convey to my readers," says Mr. Walth, "is in sharing virtues, faith, hope and humor it will deliver bounce in their steps for the journey of life. I feel I have triumphed after a long, demanding journey. I know others can also."

ACKNOWLEDGMENTS

DURING THE WRITING OF THIS BOOK, I RECEIVED MUCH HELP from my editor-in-chief, my wife Josephine, not only for typing my rough draft, but for all my life's endeavors. She caught the misspelled words in my work and removed some quotes, jokes, etc. that were repetitive.

Many of my friends suggested that I write a book and for years kept asking whether I had started to write. When they started to ask for copies of my book, I started to think about writing seriously. How do you write a joke book seriously? These same friends contributed material for this book, some of which could not be printed. The largest contribution was the encouragement they gave me.

An Acknowledgment to Two Very Special Contributors

This space is reserved for a couple of classic remarks by our two and only grandchildren.

Grandma and Grandpa were at Kirsten's home for a weekend shortly before her third birthday. Her mother Linda baked rolls for breakfast which she topped with white frosting. As we proceeded to eat our rolls, Kirsten completely scraped the frosting off her roll. I asked Kirsten, "Why are you scraping the frosting off?"

"I don't want it," she said.

Her mother explained, "That's frosting which we use on cookies, cakes and rolls."

Kirsten said, "When it's on leaves, it's bird poop."

Her remarks were spawned by an experience a week earlier while she was picking blackberries with her dad, Dan. She asked her dad, "What is that white stuff on the leaves?" Her dad told her, "That's bird poop."

My wife Jo and I went on a trip to Mainland China about four months after the Tianammen Square incident at Beijing, China. Astronaut James Irwin was the co-host on that tour. You may recall Astronaut Irwin was a driver of the Lunar Rover vehicle on the moon during the Apollo 15 moon trip. Astronaut Irwin was sharing our tour bus during our entire travel time in China, which made our trip very special.

Upon our return home, we were telling our son Dan and his wife Linda about our trip and about Astronaut Irwin. Little did we realize that the children, Kirsten, age 7, and Eric, age 4, were paying close attention to our travelog until about a month later when Eric said, "When I grow big, I'm going to be an astronaut, then the only time I have to go to work is when the moon is out."

INTRODUCTION

THE FIRST THING YOU MAY NOTICE IS THE HIGHER PRICE OF THIS book. Let me address that matter with an old expression: "You get what you pay for." Please relate this with buying oats. If you want good, clean oats, you must pay the market price. Oats that have been through the horse come cheaper.

When you live in Minnesota, it is difficult not to write Norwegian jokes, quotes, quips, etc. The Norwegian and Polish people must be the best natured people of all—the way they put up with this stuff. I'm German myself, but I take pills for that. My aim is to spawn some new ideas that work with the old.

Every time you talk or write, your mind is on parade. There is no room in this book for profanity or vulgar language. After all, you shouldn't put anything dirty on paper unless you are a canary. A person does not need profanity to round out their vocabulary. You merely add eight new words to your vocabulary every month and within a year, your friends will wonder, "Just who does he think he is?"

Over the years, we've discovered that when people think differently, they feel and act differently. It's all in controlling your thoughts. Every survival kit should include a sense of humor. It is important to use words of good taste because you might have to eat them some day.

Fortunately, while in the army, I had learned of necessity "how to banish worry and cope with stress." A strong sense of purpose and self-worth is a big help. The purpose of this book is to share some of my experiences, thoughts, beliefs and attitudes that carried me from a very humble beginning through my adult life. If I could have had the contents of this book when I was young, it could have made my journey of life more productive and easier. Life is full of golden opportunities for doing what we naturally don't want to do.

Many of the quips, quotes, anecdotes, groaners, one-liners, questions, nonsense thoughts and observations contained in this book are original. The additional material has been collected over a period of sixty years. Where the original authors are known, credit is given. I regret that credit is not attributed to authors unknown.

ABOUT AND BY THE AUTHOR

On The Lighter Side

I HAD TWO BROTHERS, AND WE EACH HAD ONE SISTER. WE HAD A very humble beginning on a South Dakota grain and livestock farm. There is something about a livestock farm that really gets to you, especially if the wind is blowing from the wrong direction.

We matured early in life because when the chips were down, you learned to be careful as to where you stepped.

My family lived through the large depression, followed by seven years of drought on a farm. Business also was bad in town. Even the diaper business hit bottom, but we knew that was saturated.

I had it rough when I was little. My parents could not afford talcum powder.

For entertainment, I recall standing in front of a mirror and making funny faces at the mirror. Now the mirror makes funny faces at me.

We were poor, yet we were always willing to share. My mother would often cook for relatives. We never pressed our guests to feel at home. We knew that if they wanted to feel at home, they would have stayed at home.

My uncle used to tell me, "There is no need to worry about your station in life. Someone will tell you where to get off," and "Don't worry about the hard times of today. Today's headlines will be wrapped around tomorrow's garbage."

At a young age, I recalled Abraham Lincoln's quote, "All men are created equal." That came as a shock to me. I realized that there was competition out there and we must start to outgrow being merely equal.

We did the only thing we knew to fight poverty. We worked. That may have been the old-fashioned way, but it seemed to work for us.

I've been asked if any big men were born in Hosmer, South Dakota. To my knowledge, only babies.

The Indian people were in South Dakota before we were. The reason they got there first is because they had reservations. There were no curse words in the Indian language. They didn't need any because there were no taxes to pay.

A small town is a place where everybody knows whose check is good and whose husband isn't. We lived four miles from Hosmer, a town that was so small we didn't even have a village idiot. We had to take turns. One day our library burned down. All the books burned — all twelve of them. Four books had not even been colored in yet. The shoe repair shop also burned. One hundred and eight soles were lost.

The old gray mare ran the town. He was as relaxed as wet spaghetti. He had nothing to get nervous about. Even on Halloween, the young guys would ease the outhouse down so it would not be damaged.

There was a Sears catalogue in every outhouse. The Sears catalogue may have motivated us to learn to read. Those were the days when the Sears catalogue was not only read, but also was used. (This comment is meaningful only to the depression generation.) We had a two-hole (side-by-side affair) outhouse. I don't think it ever was used as a duet. There were no instructions as to which hole to use. I think comfort was the determining factor.

You may have heard that life begins at forty, but we miss too much if we wait until we are forty.

You don't have to lie awake at night to succeed. Just stay awake during the day. Only in the dictionary do you find success before work.

I had a secret ambition to outsmart horses, fish and women (aiming high).

Abraham Lincoln was great and smart, not because he lived in a log cabin, but because he got out of it.

A person should not be afraid of change. After all, Adam and Eve had to turn over a new leaf. I understand Adam was the first man awarded the Oak Leaf Cluster. Adam's first day was the longest — no Eve.

Not all men are remembered for their deeds. For example, the fellow who invented the wheel did not have a spokesperson. That's why we don't know who did it. Some men are known by their deeds, others by their mortgages, and some people don't mind how bad your English is if your scotch is good.

Old jokes never die, they just smell that way.

During a fifteen-year period, I sang in a church choir. One day the choir director instructed us as follows: "The tenors will sing until we reach the gates of Hell; then you all come in." In the absence of the choir director, we also had a song leader who just loved to sing. He was always breaking out into song. He wouldn't have had to breakout if he had gotten the key.

I read where laughter is a tranquilizer with no bad side effects. So in anticipation of writing a book, I took a course on "how to become a wit." The course was a hundred dollars, but I only had fifty.

During the dust bowl days, we needed and did receive some foreign aid, the kind you get from prayer.

We did not have enough money for music lessons or for musical instruments. I did know a few fellows that fiddled around a bit.

Robin Hood never came around to help my poor family. I read that Robin Hood would steal only from the rich. The poor didn't have anything worth taking.

Poverty is what we try to conceal while we're going through it and brag about in our memoirs.

There was a sign above the door of our one-room country schoolhouse which read, "Knowledge is free, bring your own container."

Today it's hard to imagine how much a teacher could deliver in a one-room schoolhouse with thirty children and teaching all eight grades, but they did well. I can still remember some things as follows:

George Washington was most famous for his memory. They sure put up a lot of monuments to his memory. Poor old George couldn't blame his troubles on the previous administration. He had to deliver. No one party can fool all of the people all of the time; that's why we now have a two-party system. George Washington said, "I cannot tell a lie." That worked good for him. Today, George couldn't relate well with our fishermen. He couldn't even stretch the truth with his own arms. No wonder the truth hurts. You would hurt too if you got stretched so much.

Thomas Jefferson said, "Only the Republic's birthday (July 4th) merits a national holiday." Thomas Jefferson drafted most of the Declaration of Independence at Philadelphia at the age of thirty-three. Jefferson illustrated a strong interest in many aspects of science, inventions, technology, agriculture and natural history. Jefferson warned that "Those who would trade freedom for security will lose both and will deserve neither." (This statement should be a required memory work assignment for everyone in school.)

Benjamin Franklin, in his eighties, had much input into drafting the Declaration of Independence. He was still full of wisdom and mentally very alert in his eighties. At age forty-seven, Benjamin was still playing with kites. That was his first find of electricity. It came to him in a flash. At first, he didn't fully realize the importance of his discovery. He was too shocked. Thomas Edison also contributed to our technology. If it were not for Mr. Edison, we would be watching television by candlelight today.

Abraham Lincoln said, "Who's the wise guy who poured syrup on my log cabin?"

An army sergeant said, "There will always be a choice in your meals — eat it or leave it."

My elementary teacher said, "Anyone can become president of the United States of America." I didn't believe her until I actually saw the performance of some of our presidents.

When I was five years old, we had a dog. I named him Carpenter because he did odd jobs around the house. My uncle said, "That dog has such a good pedigree, if that dog could talk, he wouldn't speak to either one of us." We also had some dogs that did not have a family tree — any old tree would do. I remember one dog that didn't have a tail. A train came by before the dog got across the railroad track and cut his tail off. That damaged his carriage and totally ruined his wagon.

My sister had a cat she named Whiskers. That kitten did light mouse work. After a lingering illness, the cat died. Through her tears, my sister exclaimed, "Daddy, Daddy, Whiskers is dead."

"Don't worry," consoled my father. "Whiskers has gone to heaven to be with God."

My sister looked puzzled. She replied, "What does God want with a dead cat?" We never knew whether it was a male or female cat. You can't tell a male from a female cat by its whiskers.

My brother had a pet rooster. He named him Robinson because he crew so. My brother also had a pet capon (a neutered rooster). The capon did not crow. He had nothing to crow about.

I asked my brother at age seventy, "Don't you wish you were a barefoot boy again?" He replied, "Not with all those chickens around the yard."

The seven years of drought and crop failure was the most frustrating time of my life. Luckily, adversity had taught me to have faith in God and I somehow developed a sense of humor, which prevented me from going crazy. That very same faith and humor also helped carry me through unpleasant experiences in the South Pacific during World War II.

During those years, we really felt helpless. Something like standing between a dog and a fire hydrant. That was also the period of time that I learned it's more fun to steal a kiss than to steal second base, and that was before I talked to the big boys. Ever since then, we didn't need many cow pies for bases. Kissing is a practice that shortens your single life.

God often tries us with a little, just to see what we would do with a lot. I'm not making jokes out of life. I'm merely recognizing the ones that are there. A sense of humor reduces people and problems to their proper proportions. God gave women a sense of humor so they could better understand the jokes they married. People who know how to laugh at themselves will never cease to be amused. I still watch pretty girls go by, but I don't remember why.

Why do so many people over the age of sixty-five make such a big fuss about getting old? All it takes is a little time. I can remember when the horse wore the harness, not the passengers. Those were the days when people who wore jeans worked, and people who paid income taxes were those who could afford to pay taxes.

Today I pay the barber ten dollars for a haircut and five dollars for a finder's fee.

Nowadays, it costs about sixty dollars to have your throat painted. I can remember when we could get a whole barn painted for half that much.

I'm the metallic age — silver in my hair, gold in my teeth and lead in my pants.

Our aim in life seems to improve as we grow older, but we do run out of ammunition.

I have a friend who goes to the health clinic every three months for observation. He likes another look at the nurse.

Through the years, I never had enough beauty rest to satisfy my needs, but I managed to look young. For many years I was asked, "How do you keep looking so young?" My answer: "It's my genes. I don't wear them too tight." That worked okay for me.

You know you're getting old when instead of avoiding temptation, temptation avoids you. Growing old does not seem so bad when you consider the alternative. People don't expect you to do much work. The hardest work I do now is pushing eighty. Now people are pulling for me. They think I'm doing great just for showing up.

Things sure have changed in my lifetime. We now have mobile homes that don't move, sports clothes to work in, junk food that costs more than the real thing, sweatshirts to loaf in, and we have three times as many television sets as there are bathtubs in the United States. Just think of all those dirty people who are watching television.

After age seventy-five, a fellow slows down a little and starts to golf and bowl. I'm a better bowler than golfer. I've never lost a bowling ball. I putt like a gorilla, but I do a pretty good job at driving. I've never smashed a golf cart. I always seem to stand too close to the golf ball — after I swing. Golf is not my strong suit. Some golfers go into a sand trap with confidence. When I go in, I bring along provisions for a day, and a change of underwear and socks.

I long for the days when Uncle Sam lived within his income and without most of ours. I witnessed our civilization's growth on TV go from infancy to adultery. Congress fighting inflation is like the Mafia fighting crime. We are making more and more dollars and less and less money. I remember when inflation was something you did to a balloon. Now a big spender is a man who supports a wife and kids. Just when you think you've found a hedge against inflation, Congress decides to trim it. Trying to curb inflation by raising taxes is like giving a drunk another drink to sober him up. If inflation continues, we'll have to do some more fixing on those fixed incomes. The salary we used to dream of is one we can't live on today. Not everybody has been affected by inflation. We still have two-bit politicians.

These days everything is taxed — even our patience. Some recent laws would indicate that lawmakers stopped at the bar, but they tell us they passed the bar. With all these laws, the only place where a person is perfectly safe is under his arms.

I was a bachelor for many years, but I got tired of eating my own cooking, eating out, washing dishes and start cooking again, in that order. I met a girl that looked like a million dollars, with every penny invested in the right places. I then decided to end it all — and got married. That was the best deal I have ever made. She is the type of girl that can tell a guy to go to hell and have him look forward to the trip. She does not always treat me the way she ought to, for which I am grateful. Some girls are very hard to figure out, but it is interesting research. My wife Jo received her M.R.S. (Mrs.) degree in 1949 and received her M.A. (Ma) degree in 1952.

I had planned a complete autobiography for this section of the book, but my wife reminded me that my life really did not begin until I met her. With age, I've learned not to start a vast project with half-vast plans.

We married for good — not for better or worse. I have a good wife and I appreciate her. To show my appreciation, the only thing I have ever done behind her back is zip her up. I have my imperfections, but not once did my wife write to or call Ralph Nader about them. I say dear to my wife because I'm a friend of hers. Marriage is like my other job — it's much easier when you like the boss. The bonds of matrimony are a good investment ,if the interest is kept up. My wife and I managed to become surrounded with people who have a positive outlook. Contacts with people of high moral standards have held our standards high, providing a life triumphantly lived.

Our greatest reward in life is our son, Daniel E. Walth. This fellow was special on the day he was born and still is special today. Our daughter-in-law, Linda, came as a bonus (another special person). We feel as though as long as we have known her, she has been like our own daughter.

More joy came our way: first, a beautiful little granddaughter, Kirsten L.; then three years later, a handsome grandson, Eric D. These two are delightful and honorable in every way.

Grandma and Grandpa would be remiss if we did not add that these two children are also very intelligent and special.

A Blizzard As Found Only During The 1930's In The Western Dakotas

W E WENT THREE MILES TO A ONE-ROOM ELEMENTARY school through deep snow and cold weather. We had a good horse named Babe, and a one-horse sleigh. As the snow got deeper, the horse kept packing the snow between the sleigh runner tracks. Often neither Babe nor we could see the tracks, but our horse could feel the solid path and, therefore, did not have to struggle through the full snow depth.

One day a real strong wind came up, resulting in a severe blizzard. Our father became very worried about us (my sister, age ten, I was eight and my brother was six). Dad decided to come for us with the larger two-horse sled. In the meantime, we left school for the three-mile trip home. We could not see where to make our turns. I remembered my dad often told us, "If you ever get into a situation on the way home that your horse does not want to turn at your command, just forget about driving the horse. You may be lost, the horse is not, and he wants to get home as much as you do. Let Babe take you home." She did take us to within a quarter of a mile from our farm and stopped. There we saw Dad with his two horses and sled. His team didn't know about the snow-packed path. They broke through the deep snow and started to hump. They broke the harness and one horse was down in the deep snow trying to get up. Dad's team was far enough off our packed track so that we managed to get by. We kids stopped and helped Dad and his horses get home. We left his big sled in the deep snow until the snow melted down to a manageable depth. One Saturday afternoon about six weeks later, Dad and I went after the sled.

We all must have been candidates for hypothermia. It was good that we didn't know what that was in those days.

Eager To Earn Some Spending Money For The Coming Years

A T THE AGE OF SIXTEEN AND EAGER TO EARN SOME SPENDING money, I headed for the Red River Valley of Minnesota to hand pick and bag potatoes. The workdays were from sunrise to sunset every day. Board and room was included, consisting of sleeping in a hayloft in the barn and three meals a day that left me hungry enough to eat raw potatoes in the field every day. After two months, I came home very tired but sixty dollars richer (a dollar a day).

I used the sixty dollars to buy four wild horses from a trucker who obtained the wild horses west of Mobridge, South Dakota, through Indians who rounded them up for him. Those horses had never seen people close up before. They would bite, kick and strike with their front feet. We managed to tie them up to a strong manger in stalls and carried their water and feed to them. Within a month, I broke three of them to saddle. After they were well saddlebroken, my dad took one of his large, heavy horses and helped me put the harness on a bronco, and tied the bronco securely to the gentle horse, hitched them as a team onto a stone boat containing a couple of large rocks and drove around the fields and pasture. We adjusted the eveners so the bronco had to pull more than his share. After the bronco was so tired he could hardly walk, he was very manageable. So were the other two broncos after going through the same sessions.

The fourth bronco was such that Dad wanted to shoot him. By then, I had already sold two of the broncos — one for $175 and another for $200, which was a gain of $160 on one and $185 on the other. That was much better than picking potatoes for a dollar a day. I just had to save the fourth bronco.

One Saturday, Dad went to town with a sleigh. After Dad was about a half mile from home, I thought, now is the time to break that mean bronco before the horse gets shot. Said horse was tied in a narrow stall next to the door of the barn. The snow in the yard was a good three to four-foot deep, which was in my favor because the horse would tire faster.

The main part was to get the saddle on tight. I managed to get the saddle on him. He tried to buck the saddle off while he was tied to the stall. After about a ten-minute struggle to get the saddle off, the bronco settled down enough for me to get the bridle on him. The bit in his mouth was something new for him and the bronco then had his attention on the bit. That allowed me time to untie him from the manger and get myself into the saddle. This was the critical part. He did not raise up and start bucking until we were out in the yard (that was a relief). That horse snorted, went in circles, went head up high, then head down, all while he was turning. After the first good leap, I felt my cap coming off (it was a tied, tight-fitting hunting cap with earflaps). At about that time, I heard my mother screaming near the house. After a while, I got so tired that one more good jump and turn would throw me off. The bronco stopped bucking and stood in place, rocking like a rocking chair, which I enjoyed. My mother came over. She had seen my cap come off, so she brought the cap, walked up to the horse to hand it to me, and the bronco did not respond to her coming near. I now had my cap and had caught my breath.

The next move was to ride the horse. I asked my mother to get the riding whip, and we were off. I rode that horse four miles north and back. Then I decided to go after the mail before my dad got to the mailbox on his way home (one mile south of the farm). At the mailbox, I had to get off the horse to reach the mail. I had the pleasant surprise of getting back on the horse and getting a horseback ride home with the mail. That horse never bucked or even acted up again. Within six months, I sold that horse for $250 and was sorry I sold it. It was a beautiful horse and turned out to be a good horse.

Memories Of A Seven-Year Drought And Seven Years Of Crop Failure In South Dakota During The 1930's

THE HOSMER, SOUTH DAKOTA REGION OF THE UNITED STATES is a place mostly inhabited by people who, by circumstances of inheritance, came here. Our ancestors homesteaded the land and many stayed. They and their homes were closely bound to the land. It was theirs. The hard times gave them spiritual growth. They always talked in terms of next year — next year will be better.

People who lived in the Dakotas saw things you don't see when driving through at sixty-five miles per hour. We saw the way the native grass grows back after a dry period and how healthy livestock can be when eating native grass only. Imagine the solitude and silence of the plains, the landscape of earth, blue sky and green grass. These things must be the attraction for many.

Some people have come to love living under the large sky, its winds and storms, knowing that its loneliness is an honest reflection on the people's willingness to accept the lifestyle with realism, not despair.

The people of the Great Plains are most hospitable. Many have little but are willing to share what they have. This may have developed because they needed each other in order to survive, not necessarily are they kinder and have more love for one another. They, too, gossip, pigeonhole people and take them for granted, yet, overall, there seems to be healthier conditions toward deeper love and support in times of need.

I recall the hot forty-mile-an-hour winds that continually howled for four days or more. These winds drew the moisture out of the ground, turning fields into dust that destroyed an entire crop within a few days. Many families abandoned their farms and moved out of the region, leaving behind not only the furniture in the house but china and handmade quilts, even family photographs. These moves were painful.

There is not much written about the Dakotas' drought period. It may be because it was so hard to live through. People had no desire to talk about it, much like not wanting to talk about your army experiences in a war zone. Perhaps it will be many more years before the entire story of those days will be told. The dust bowl stories contain some of the best theology I know.

My parents had to mortgage the farm with the Federal Land Bank and spend the proceeds for grain, seed, feed for livestock and operating costs to till the land every year, and did not receive a harvest. There was no potential in sight for this designated farmer. That was a lonely feeling of being friendless, sort of a homesickness coming over me while at home.

There was always work to do. We merely held on to the farm. There was almost a complete absence of social life. I could not go on to school after grade school graduation because our operation was too large a job for my father and mother alone. Hired farm hands were available for thirty dollars a month, plus board and room, but we didn't have thirty dollars. It was tradition that the oldest son would work and preserve the farm that would be his some day (just another dream).

The absence of formal schooling appears not to have been a lasting handicap today, although I had experienced some psychological trauma for many years. After my discharge from the U.S. Army (WWII), I went to a business college under the GI Bill. The VA education bill was the best thing ever provided for a veteran. My goal was to acquire everything I wanted out of life without violating the rights of others. That, I believe, is a true measure of success.

I had no desire to farm in South Dakota. After completing my education following World War II, I worked for the Minneapolis Star and Tribune in circulation. I also sold insurance, then went into the farm equipment and motor truck dealership partnership in New Prague, Minnesota. For the past thirty years, my wife and I have been in the real estate business in Rochester, Minnesota.

Although my wife and I are no longer very active in real estate, we remain vigorously active and usefully productive. We have had some health problems but feel genuinely happy, fulfilled and trust that God and the Mayo Clinic will keep us going. Even today, farmers and small town people suffer in silence and despair as they see a family move away, eroding the tax base and putting another unsaleable house on the market.

The frontier often has been romanticized in the United States culture by movies and novels glorifying the violent West.

COLLECTIONS AND OBSERVATIONS

Officer: "I'm looking for a small man with one eye."

Ole: "Since he is a small man, wouldn't it be better to use both eyes looking for him?"

~

Ad in a local paper: Attractive, unattached, single kitten seeks position in a little girl's lap. Will also do light mouse work.

~

A good storyteller is a person who had a good memory and hopes that other people haven't.

~

Talk is cheap because the supply is much greater than the demand.

~

Helga: "I wonder why they took Lawrence Welk off of TV."

Lena: "I suppose because there was too much sax and violins."

~

Some of the best boy scouts are girls.

~

I let my wife spend money like water — drip, drip, drip.

~

Young mother: "Doctor, my baby swallowed an ounce of castor oil, what should I do?"

Doctor: "Just keep him quiet and don't point him at anyone."

~

Clifford: "What's that crawling up the wall?"

Harry: "A ladybug."

Clifford: "Wow, what eyesight."

~

Wife on the phone: "Dear, I can't get the car started. I think the carburetor is flooded."

Husband: "Where is the car?"

Wife: "In the lake."

~

Alex: "It's hard whistling at those hot pants when your tongue is hanging out."

~

Girls prefer the simple things in life — men.

~

When I was a little boy the only teacher strikes we had were inflicted on unruly students.

~

Ole had a peach of a secretary. Lena canned her.

~

One good thing about being poor — it's inexpensive.

~

When run-down, the best thing to take is the license number.

~

Beethoven's fifth is not something to drink.

~

Ole: "I'd give five thousand dollars to anyone who would do my worrying for me."
Sven: "You've hired yourself a worrier. Where's the five thousand dollars?"
Ole: "That's your first worry."

~

There is one thing to say about nudists — you can't pin anything on them.

~

Even the fashion editors don't know what the miniskirt will be up to next.

~

I read about the sultan who had a harem and each day he sent a trusted servant to fetch a wife that was most appropriate for the task at hand. The sultan lived to be ninety-seven; the servant died at age forty. Moral: It's running after the women that kills you.

~

Roland: "A woman drove me to drink. I feel bad because I never wrote to thank her."

~

Gus says you can't stop folks from thinking, so now let's try to get them to start.

~

The father of nine kids panicked when his wife told him, "Monday is Labor Day."

~

Stopping at a wayside service station, the lady motorist inquired timidly, "Do you have a rest room?" "Nope," replied the attendant, "when any of us gets tired, we just sit on one of those oil drums."

~

Roland's song: "I found my still on blueberry hill."

~

Boy: "Work is something that other people think of for you to do. Play is what you think of yourself."

~

Doctor: "You drink a lot, don't you?"
Patient: "No, I spill most of it."

~

Christmas is the time when gals get "Santamental."

~

Ours is the only nation where recipients of a relief check drive up in private automobiles.

~

Roland: "Could you lend me ten dollars to buy some groceries?"
Alex: "How do I know you won't use the money to buy a bottle of whiskey?"
Roland: "I've already got the money for the whiskey."

~

The moron wanted to die in church, so he shot himself in the temple.

~

Clifford says, "When a gal comes along with a nice build, Alex wants to be a building inspector."

~

Even children with perfect table manners will spill the beans now and then.

~

Traveling salesman to waitress: "Two eggs so hard they have plastic edges, two pieces of burnt toast, and a cup of cold coffee."
Waitress: "Anything else?"
Salesman: "Yes, sit down and nag me — I'm homesick."

~

Playing with commas: "Woman without her man, is lost." "Woman, without her, man is lost."

~

Farm equipment dealer: "We sell everything the farmer uses except profanity, and if you use our equipment, you won't need that."

~

Headline: "Father of eleven fined nine hundred dollars for failing to stop."

~

Lulu says she would rather be flat broke than flat busted.

～

It isn't what the children know that bothers parents. It's how they found out.

～

Hotel manager: "Did you find any of our towels in that man's suitcase?"
Hotel detective: "No, but I found a chambermaid in his grip."

～

Ella: "I caught my husband flirting."
Maggie: "That's the way I caught mine, too."

～

Lincoln walked nine miles to get a book to read. Now, in honor of his birthday, the libraries are closed.

～

If Ralph Nader ever became a father, I bet he would return the baby for seat covers.

～

The speaker was wound up, but I don't think his watch was.

～

Sophie: "Is your new boyfriend a lady-killer?"
Lulu: "He sure is. He starves them to death."

～

People do funny things — like protecting ducks so they can shoot them.

～

Women are like ships — if kept in good shape and painted, they remain see worthy.

～

Sophie: "Why did you get drunk in the first place?"
Clifford: "I didn't, it was the last place where I got drunk."

～

If it weren't for installment plans, a lot of animals would still be around wearing their own fur.

～

Wife to salesman husband: "I always worry when you are away from home."
Husband: "But angel, I'll be back before you know it."
Wife: "That's what worries me."

~

Bob Hope said: "A politician is a person who works his gums before election and gums the works after election."

~

A man inspected his wife's new bathing suit and remarked: "It's just big enough to prevent you from being tanned where you ought to be.

~

A Scotsman's experience was very embarrassing. He would have sworn the sign on the door read "Laddies."

~

Professor: "Every morning I take a cold shower, a brisk rub down, and feel rosy all over."
Student: "Tell us more about Rosy."

~

Lady driver: "Do you charge batteries here?"
Harvey: "We sure do."
Lady: "Good, then put a new one in this car and charge it to my husband."

~

"Is your daddy at home, son?"
"No sir. He hasn't been home since Mother saw Santa Claus kissing the maid."

~

Uncle Tom to little girl: "What will you do when you get as big as your mother?"
Little Girl: "Diet."

~

On the first day of school, the teacher explained that if anyone had to go to the washroom, they should hold up two fingers. One puzzled boy plaintively asked, "How is that going to help?"

~

Johnny: "Why does the whistle blow for a fire?"
Billy: "It doesn't blow for the fire, it blows for water. They've got the fire."

~

Two ladies were indulging in pie and ice cream. One said that she had to watch her waistline. The other purred, "And how lucky you are to have it right out there where you can see it."

~

John: "I started out on the theory that the world had an opening for me."

George: "And you found it?"

John: "I sure did. Nobody could be further in the hole than I am."

~

The wife you save may be your own. Buy her a washing machine.

~

Doctor: "I'm operating on a fellow who had a golf ball knocked down his throat."

Nurse: "Who is the man waiting? A relative?"

Doctor: "No, that's the golfer. He's waiting for his golf ball."

~

Father: "When I was a boy, I thought nothing of a ten-mile walk."

Son: "I don't think much of it myself."

~

Old-timer looking at a sign in a country store window that read: Ladies ready to wear clothes. "It's about time," he said.

~

Johnny was gazing at his one-week-old brother squealing in his crib.

"Did he really come from heaven?" inquired Johnny.

"Yes dear," said his mother.

"No wonder they put him out," said Johnny.

~

The lady of the house was showing the new maid the premises and said, "This dining room set goes back to Louis the 14th."

"Don't feel bad," said the maid. "My whole living room set goes back to Sears on the 15th unless I make all the back payments."

~

Bill: "What do you think of tight skirts?"

Tom: "I think that women ought to leave liquor alone."

~

The teacher wrote on the blackboard: I ain't had no fun all summer. Then she asked a small boy in the front row, "William, what should I do to correct this?"

"Maybe get a boyfriend," he suggested helpfully.

~

Boy: "My dad's an Elk, a Lion and a Moose."

Girl: "What does it cost to see him?"

~

A pessimist is a woman driver who is sure she can't park her car in a tight place. An optimist is a husband who thinks she won't try.

~

Army doctor: "Do you have any physical defects?"
Draftee: "Yes sir! No guts."

~

Roland: "What do you think would go well with my new purple and green socks?"
Harry: "Hip boots."

~

Sign: No trespassing — survivors will be prosecuted.

~

Roland: "How do porcupines make love?"
Gus: Very carefully.

~

He: "I'm chilled to the bone."
She: "Why don't you put on your cap?"

~

Rosie: "Aren't you getting Johnny and Bill confused?"
Mary: "Yes, I get Johnny confused one night and Bill the next night."

~

Alex: "She sure gave you a dirty look."
Gus: "Who?"
Alex: "Mother Nature."

~

Eric's young sister came to the schoolhouse door and handed the following note to the teacher. Teacher, please excuse Eric. He caught a skunk.

~

Father: "Remember, my boy, beauty is only skin deep."
Son: "Deep enough for me. I'm not a cannibal."

~

A cannibal mother was ex-plaining to her children while all were watching an airplane flying over, "It's something like a coconut, you just eat what's inside."

~

Harry: "Your pants look sad."
Gus: "What do you mean?"
Harry: "Sort of depressed."

~

Lulu: "Waltz faster, dear. This is a rumba."

~

Little Marvin's remark on finding a button in his salad: "I suppose it fell off while the salad was dressing.

~

I talked to Roland the other day. He was quite a mess. He had proposed to three girls, told his boss off, sold his car, then the army turned him down.

~

The proud mother was exhibiting her baby to friends. "He's just doing fine. He's eating solids now — newspapers, pencils, keys ..."

~

Mr. Johnson: "Jones tried to beat a train to the crossing."
Mr. Van: "Did he get across?"
Mr. Johnson: "No, but they're making one for him."

~

Ole: "We must think of the future. We ought to economize more. If I were to die, where would you be?"
Lena: "The question is, where would you be?"

~

She was barefoot up to her chin.

~

Employer to beautiful girl who filed a job application: "Miss Jones, under Experience, you could be a little more specific than just oh boy."

~

Wife: "I broke my husband of biting his nails."
Friend: "How?"
Wife: "I hid his teeth."

~

Willy asked an explorer, "Will wild beasts in the jungle harm you if you carry a torch?"
Explorer: "It all depends on how fast you carry it."

~

Teacher: "Name five things that contain milk."
Little Sven: "Butter, cheese, ice cream, and two cows."

~

Ella: "Jack makes me tired."
Maggie: "It's your own fault. You should stop running after him."

~

The clothes that keep a man looking his best are worn by girls on beaches.

~

Small boy: "Daddy, did Mr. Edison make the first talking machine?"
Father: "No, son, the creator performed that feat in the Garden of Eden, but Mr. Edison made the first one that could be shut off."

~

Feed your cat lemons and you'll have a sour puss.

~

A bus driver was filling out a report about a highway breakdown. When he came to the line Disposition of Passengers, he wrote mad as hornets.

~

I read that rubbing elbows with a man will reveal things about a person that you never knew be-fore. I wonder if the same applies to rubbing fenders.

~

Arthur: "I was born an Englishman, I have lived as an Englishman, and I hope to die an Englishman."
Max: "Have you no ambition at all?"

~

Two drunks were walking down the railroad tracks. First Drunk: "Gee, this is a long stairway."
Second drunk: "I wouldn't mind the long stairway if the handrails weren't so low."

~

I know a place where women don't wear anything except a string of beads.
Gee, where's that?
Around their necks.

~

There is a new TV serial. The characters are all hippies — sort of a no-soap opera.

~

If I told you that you have a beautiful and lovely body, would you hold it against me?

~

Harry: "Does the moon affect the tide?"
Ella: "No, only the untied."

~

Teacher: "Can anyone in this class tell me why an Indian wears feathers in his hair?"
Eric: "Sure, to keep his wig-wam."

~

Boasted the Virginian: "One of my ancestors signed the Declaration of Independence."

"Indeed," replied the Jewish fellow. "One of mine signed the Ten Commandments."

≈

Vegetables keep you trim — if you grow them yourself.

≈

A woman clad in a suit jacket and slip approached the lost and found department and inquired anxiously, "Has anybody turned in a black skirt with five children from two to six hanging on it?"

≈

Speaking of being considerate, I always oil the lawn mower for my wife every Saturday before I go out to play golf.

≈

Diplomats are frequently decor-ated in European countries. We'd like to crown some of ours.

≈

The sap runs in the spring but the girls catch him just the same.

≈

Why shouldn't eighteen-year-olds vote? There'll never be another time when they know everything.

≈

Orator: "All I am I owe to my dear old mother."

Heckler: "Why don't you give her the twenty-five cents?"

≈

The first signs of spring are the blooming idiots on the highways.

≈

Some girls dressed in slacks and sweaters look like they are smugg-ling cannonballs through the con-federate lines.

≈

There is nothing like a hard horseback ride to make a fellow feel better off.

≈

Maggie: "What position does your boyfriend play on the football team?"

Lulu: "He's one of the drawbacks, I think."

≈

If the court ruled that there must be some chicken in what is offered to the public as chicken soup, what is the ruling on hot dogs?

~

A nifty young gal walked into the drugstore and whispered, "Do you have any Lifeboy?" Imagine her surprise when Alex replied, "Set the pace, set the pace!"

~

A sign in a western state reads: 4,229 people died of gas in this state last year. Two inhaled it, 27 put a lighted match to it, and 4,200 stepped on it.

~

Cop to a staggering man at 3:00 a.m.: "Where are you going at this time of night?"
Man: "To a lecture."

~

A young lady was insulted when the bill collector asked, "Do you owe any back house rent?" She said, "I'll have you know we have plumbing inside."

~

Quite often a girl gets rid of a headache by telling him she has one.

~

There was a man standing in the middle of a pasture with a rope in his hand. He could not remember whether he found a rope or lost a horse.

~

Gratitude can change our common days into Thanksgiving, ordinary jobs into joy, and ordinary opportunities into blessings.

~

Some men have a den in their house to growl in.

~

Some cocktails make you see double and feel single.

~

Mary: "I wonder what men talk about when they're off by themselves."
Nellie: "Probably the same things we do."
Mary: "Oh, aren't they awful."

~

Sunday school teacher: "Who led the children of Israel out of Egypt?"
Boy: "It wasn't me, ma'am. We just moved here from Chicago last month."

~

Son: "Daddy, I'll tell you what the ice man said to Mama if you give me a dime."
Dad: "Okay, here's your dime."
Son: "He said, 'Any ice today, lady?' "

~

Girl in the rear of bus to driver: "Wait just a minute while I get my clothes off." Every head in the bus swung around to see a girl step off the bus carrying two packages of laundry.

~

An actor believes that a small role is better than a long loaf.

~

You can get a chicken dinner for ten cents at any feed store. Chickens don't each much.

~

Oscar: "My grandfather lived to be ninety and never used glasses."
Roland: "Well, lots of people prefer to drink from a bottle."

~

A fire in a backstage ladies dressing room was put out in ten minutes, but it took two hours to put out the firemen.

~

Visitor to little boy: "What are you going to be if the neighbors let you grow up?"

~

Paul: "It's getting awfully late and we haven't hit a duck yet."
Gus: "Let's miss two more and then go home."

~

Wife: "Doctor, I want the truth. Is there no hope for my husband?"
Doctor: "Madam, I'm afraid he can't recover, but to make sure, I'm going to call in another doctor."

~

Teacher: "How much is three times three?"
Eric: "Nine."
Teacher: "That's pretty good."
Eric: "Pretty good? Say it's perfect."

~

A fellow fell out of a third story window. An officer walked up and asked him, "What happened?" The fellow said, "I don't know. I just got here."

~

Grease in a car can cause friction between owner and serviceman if it gets on the upholstery.

≈

≈

Customer at a cafe: "Do you serve crabs here?"
Waitress: "Yes, sir. We serve anyone."

≈

Doctor: "Your leg is swollen, but I wouldn't worry about it."
Patient: "If your leg was swollen, I wouldn't worry about it either."

≈

Waiter: "Do you want this pizza cut into six or eight pieces?"
Customer: "Cut it into six pieces, I don't think I can eat eight."

≈

Wife: "These flowers will grow faster if you talk to them."
Husband: "But I don't know how to talk geranium."

≈

If the justice department does not make any improvements, our police department may not continue to have a listed telephone number.

≈

During a Christmas play, not a preacher was stirring, not even a mouse.

Patient: "Doctor, do I have to give up tobacco, wine, women and song?"
Doctor: "You may sing all you want to."

≈

Roland: "My uncle was a great politician."
Clifford: "What did he run for?"
Roland: "The border."

≈

Little Dora: "I was playing postman."
Mother: "How could you play postman when you don't have any letters?"
Little Dora: "I found a bunch of letters in your trunk tied together with a pretty ribbon, and I posted one in everyone's mailbox on this block."

≈

In times like these, it helps to remember that there have always been times like these.

≈

Sunday school teacher: "What do you think a land flowing with milk and honey will be like?"
Little Kirsten: "Sticky."

~

Sign outside a psychiatrist's office: Two couches, no waiting.

~

What this country needs is a good five-cent nickel.

~

I do most of my work sitting down — that's where I shine.

~

Running into debt is generally followed by running into creditors.

~

Gus: "I understand you have a speaking acquaintance with her."
Alex: "Merely a listening acquaintance."

~

Preacher: "Who do you know that is perfect?"
Little man: "My wife's first husband."

~

Some realtors have lots to be thankful for.

~

Cutting off a mule's ears will not make him a horse.

~

If you can't afford that operation now, you'll have to talk about the old one another year.

~

A lecture can make you feel numb at one end and dumb at the other.

~

Roland's speech had a happy ending. Everyone was glad it was over.

~

Elderly lady to pastor: "Knowing that you don't eat sweets, I'm sending candy to your wife and nuts to you."

~

Son: "Dad, will you help me find the least common denominator in this problem?"
Dad: "Good heavens, son, they were looking for that when I was a kid. Hasn't that been found yet?"

~

Speaker: "After an introduction like that, I can hardly wait to hear what I'm going to say."

~

Witness: "Well, I think ..."
Lawyer: "Don't think! In this courtroom, you are to tell what you know, not what you think."
Witness: "Well, I'm not a lawyer. I can't talk without thinking."

~

Policeman: "I'm looking for a man with one eye named Carnell."
Bystander: "What's the other eye called?"

~

Roland reading names on gravestones: Here lies a lawyer and a good man. "Imagine," said Roland, "two men buried in the same grave."

~

Boy: "Oh, look at that cow and the calf rubbing noses. That sight makes me want to do the same."
Girl: "Well, go ahead — it's your cow."

~

Roland: "The policeman shot my dog."
Gus: "Was he mad?"
Roland: "Well, he wasn't too pleased about it."

~

A cannibal chief had captured a man near his camp and said to the man, "What is your profession?"
The man replied, "I was editor of my company paper."
"Good," smiled the cannibal chief, "tomorrow you'll be editor-in-chief."

~

After Dutch treat on everything on a date, the girl responded to her escort, "Since we've gone Dutch on everything else, you can just kiss yourself goodnight."

~

Boy: "You know, sweetheart, since I met you, I can't eat, sleep or drink."
Girl: "Why not?"
Boy: "I'm broke."

~

Girl: "Would you like to take a walk?"
Boy: "I'd love to."
Girl: "Well, don't let me detain you."

~

Conceited: "I can tell just by looking into a girl's eyes exactly how she feels about me."
Girl: "Gee, that must be embarrassing for you."

~

Boy: "You look prettier every minute. Do you know what that's a sign of?"
Girl: "Yes, you're about to run out of gas."

~

Boy (with one hand cupped over the other): "If you can guess what I have in my hand, I'll take you out tonight."
Girl: "An elephant!"
Boy: "Nope, but that's close enough. I'll stop for you at 7:00 p.m."

~

Boy: "Do you think you could be happy with a guy like me?"
Girl: "Perhaps, if he isn't too much like you."

~

Girl: "Do you love me?"
Boy: "Yes, dear."
Girl: "Would you die for me?"
Boy: "No, mine is an undying love."

~

Bill: "That girl in the red dress isn't very smart."
Sam: "I know. She hasn't paid any attention to me, either."

~

Boy: "What must I give you for one little kiss?"
Girl: "Chloroform!"

~

What came first, the chicken or the egg? The chicken, of course. God couldn't lay an egg.

~

Everyone sat down at the dinner table. Mother noticed something missing. Mother said, "Susan, you forgot to put a knife and fork at Uncle Joe's place."
"I didn't think he needed them," exclaimed Susan. "Daddy said he always eats like a horse."

~

Man: "I'm sorry I can't come to your party this evening. I have an engagement to see *Romeo and Juliet*."
Woman: "That's okay. Bring them along, too."

~

An Indian chief named Running Water had two daughters name Hot and Cold, and a son named Luke.

~

A little bird told me so.
It must have been a stool pigeon.

≈

On the first day of spring, my true love gave to me — five packs of seed, four sacks of fertilizer, three cans of weed killer, two bottles of insect spray, and a pruning knife for the pear tree.

≈

There is a world of difference between the North and South Poles.

≈

Kirsten: "What goes ha, ha, ha, ha, ha, plop?"
Eric: "Someone laughing his head off."

≈

Customer: "Waiter, there's no chicken in my chicken soup."
Waiter: "There's no horse in the horseradish either."

≈

Boss: "Jones, how long have you been working here?"
Jones: "Ever since I heard you coming down the hall."

≈

The latest electric ranges include venetian blinds on the oven door for bashful girls who bake rump roast.

≈

A native of a tourist area was asked: "How is business?"
Native: "Tourists come with a twenty dollar bill and a pair of shorts and don't change either one."

≈

It's raining cats and dogs outside.
Yeah, I know, I just stepped in a poodle.

≈

He has more pull than my dentist.

≈

Small boy: "Dad, may I have two dollars?"
Dad: "Son, you must learn the value of a dollar."
Son: "I know the value of a dollar, Dad. That's why I asked for two."

≈

The best cure for water on the brain is a tap on the head.

≈

Lena: "Why does she let all the boys kiss her?"
Lulu: "She once slapped a guy who was chewing tobacco."

≈

First golfer: "You almost hit my wife."

Second golfer: "Did I? Well, have a shot at mine."

~

Lulu: "There we sat under the moon, and he just sat there making wishes."

~

Wife: "When I'm down in the dumps, I buy myself a new hat."

Husband: "I wondered where you got them."

~

One cute little thing said to another, "All a sweater does for me is make me itch."

~

Clifford: "Did Sophie blush when her shoulder strap broke?"

Gus: "I didn't notice."

~

All it takes to feather your nest these days is a little down.

~

He is as nervous as a long-tailed cat in a room full of rocking chairs.

~

Pete: "My wife insists that gasoline and alcohol don't mix."

Roland: "Oh, they do mix, but they don't taste good."

~

"Dad, when I go to college, I'll need an encyclopedia."

"Encyclopedia, nothing. You'll walk to classes like the other boys."

~

Census taker: "How many bushels of corn did you raise last year?"

Backwoodsman: "I didn't bushel it, I bottled it."

~

He: "What is home without a mother?"

"I am tonight," replied the cute little blond.

~

"I wouldn't vote for you if you were St. Peter."

"If I were St. Peter, you couldn't vote for me. You wouldn't be in my precinct."

~

John: "My girlfriend is a twin."

Joe: "How do you tell them apart?"

John: "Her brother is built different."

~

How do you make a peach cordial?
You buy her a couple of drinks.

~

Gus: "Do you believe in clubs for women?"
Roland: "Yes, when kindness fails."

~

Doctor: "You have acute appendicitis."
Lady: "Listen, doctor, I came here to be examined, not admired."

~

Sometimes a woman doesn't care for a man's company unless he owns it.

~

She: "Why does the umpire wear that funny wire thing over his face?"
He: "To keep him from biting the ballplayers, dear."

~

An auction is the only place where you can get something for nodding.

~

Lulu: "I like men with blue eyes and greenbacks."

~

Boss: "Smith, I found a bottle of rye and ginger ale in your desk. What do you make of it?"
Smith: "Highballs."

~

Ernest: "How can I drive a nail without hitting my finger?"
Roland: "Let your wife hold the nail."

~

The girl had a mink coat, a new sports car, a Persian rug, all designer clothes and a built-in bar. To think that five years ago her teacher flunked that gal in math.

~

A fellow from way back in the hills died upon seeing his first automobile. He didn't see it soon enough.

~

Patient: "What do my reports show, doctor?"
Doctor: "According to our analysis, there is a small percentage of blood getting into your alcohol system."

~

Her face is her fortune, and it runs into a nice figure.

~

Johnny to teacher: "I don't want to scare you, but Pop said if I didn't get better grades, somebody is going to get a spanking."

~

Telephone operator: "I'm sorry, sir, that number has been taken out."
Caller: "Oh, is that so? Well, can you give me any information as to just who has taken her out?"

~

Officer: "Slow down that truck. Haven't you got a governor on it?"
Jake: "No sir, the governor is in the state capital. That's fertilizer you smell."

~

A man who crosses the ocean twice without taking a bath is a dirty double crosser.

~

Lulu: "I have an awful lot of electricity in my hair."
Maggie: "No wonder you have such shocking things on your mind."

~

A gold digger is a girl who will date any man who can pass the asset test.

~

Fred: "Her niece is rather good looking."
Joe: "Don't say knees is, say knees are."

~

Lulu thought assets were little donkeys.

~

Lulu says it's better to have loved a short man than not to have loved a-tall.

~

Roland saw the sun go down and stayed up all night trying to figure out where it went. Finally it dawned on him.

~

Lulu: "I stood him up at the party, but he kept falling down."

~

A young woman resigned as governess because of a backward child and a forward father.

~

A lady is a woman who makes it easy for a man to be a gentleman.

~

The average girl would rather have beauty than brains because the average man can see better than he can think.

∼

Lulu: "It's shameful the way you start making passes at me after six drinks."
Roland: "What's shameful about that?"
Lulu: "Wasting five drinks."

∼

Father: "What are your young man's intentions?"
Lily: "Well, Daddy, he's keeping me pretty much in the dark."

∼

Plastic surgeons can do almost anything with a nose, except keep it out of other people's business.

∼

A tenderfoot is a person who rides a horse and finds out that his feet are not so tender after all.

∼

Pasteurized milk does not always come from pastured cows.

∼

Teacher: "Johnny, can you tell me where the Red Sea is?"
Johnny: "Yes, ma'am, it's on the third line of my report card."

∼

On your tax return, you may not deduct hair tonic as overhead.

∼

Toast: To the ladies who kindle the only flame firemen cannot extinguish and against which there is no insurance coverage.

∼

On their birthday, some men take a day off and some women take a year off.

∼

It's as easy to become intoxicated on water as it is on land.

∼

Some of the jokes appearing in this book made me kick a few slats out of my cradle when I first heard them. That's old!

∼

Gus says a party is where your wife gives her friends better food than she gives you.

~

President: "You misunderstood me. I asked only the board, not the bored, to remain after the meeting.

~

Gus says a woman who doesn't gossip has no friends to speak of.

~

The better a woman looks, the longer a man does.

~

The doctor told Roland to slow down, so he is now chasing older women.

~

Why are all dumb-blond jokes one-liners? So men can understand them.

~

What is the difference between government bonds and men? Government bonds mature.

~

Always give a woman driver at least half the road; that is, if you can tell which half she wants.

~

A driver hit three parked cars, two light poles, and one telephone pole, then lost control.

~

One sure way to test your will power is to see a friend with a black eye and not ask any questions.

~

There are some nuts rattling around inside automobiles that the manufacturer did not put there.

~

Some people drive like tomorrow is not worth waiting for.

~

Just because you see its tracks is no sign that a train has just passed.

~

People who drive very fast may get where they're going ahead of time. Sometimes forty or fifty years ahead of time.

~

When mending their ways, most people don't use heavy enough thread.

~

A Sunday golfer is a person who is more interested in a hole-in-one than in the Holy One.

≈

A sure way to make relatives feel at home is to visit them at their home.

≈

Much of science is trained and organized common sense.

≈

Corn cannot be raised on the moon, but the moon is great for raising taxes.

≈

A sleepwalker is a person who gets his rest and his exercise at the same time.

≈

We have more people spilling the beans than we have raising beans.

≈

If you think a woman can't keep a secret, ask her age.

≈

More people are thoughtless than speechless.

≈

Death and taxes are inevitable, but death is not a repeater.

≈

The phone is probably out of order when a woman suffers in silence.

≈

The reason Rip Van Winkle could sleep for twenty years was the fact that none of his neighbors had a lawn mower, radio or television set.

≈

The creatures that sleep standing up are horses and fathers of one-month-old babies.

≈

Wear a smile. It does not wear out, never goes up or down in price, never is taxed, and improves your appearance. How's that for a face-lift?

≈

If you don't have prejudices, people may think you don't understand our social system.

≈

If you would rather pinch pennies than pinch a girl, you are stingy.

≈

A secret is usually something that is told to only one person at a time.

~

Everything we have is taxed — even our patience.

~

Within one year, three million kids will turn sixteen, and six million parents will turn pale.

~

Many teenage boys who take an aptitude test find they are well suited for retirement.

~

Blessed are the teenagers for they shall inherit the national debt.

~

Robert had a telephone installed so he could hang up on people.

~

The first telephone had cranks on them. They still do.

~

The world needs less television and more vision, then maybe the kids would be as well adjusted as the TV set.

~

I remember when the only bad thing on television was the reception.

~

If TV doesn't improve, husbands may go back to listening to their wives.

~

Television opens many doors, mostly on refrigerators.

~

If you feel that you have all the world's problems, just listen to the TV soaps.

~

Little boys and little girls who continually interrupt may grow up and make a fortune doing TV commercials.

~

A pedestrian must learn to think fast on his feet.

~

The hazard in smoking a pipe is high blood pressure from trying to keep it lit.

~

When some folks yell for tolerance, what they really want are special privileges.

~

Go slow. This is a one-hearse town.

~

Traffic lights are what give pedestrians so much confidence that they never see who or what hit them.

~

An unemployed schoolteacher has no principal nor class.

~

A pretty girl has a choice of vacation spots. She can go to the mountains and see the scenery or go to the beach and be the scenery.

~

The best place to spend your vacation is just inside your income.

~

Vision is definitely affected by glasses, especially after they've been filled and emptied several times.

~

This world needs guns of smaller caliber and men of larger caliber.

~

A political war is one in which people shoot from the lips.

~

I read that a confession is good for the soul. In Washington, a confession can be turned into a best seller.

~

The sophisticated equipment of today's weatherman is what enables him to explain in greater detail why he was wrong.

~

Ole reports that Lena thinks swimming is good for his health. She's always telling him to go jump into the river.

~

The successful man has a wife who tells him what to do and a secretary who does it.

~

An unusual amount of common sense is sometimes called wisdom.

~

Girls have an unfair advantage over men. If they can't get what they want by being smart, they get it by being dumb.

≈

A bargain sale is where women fight for merchandise that's been reduced in price because nobody wanted it in the first place.

≈

Not all people repeat rumors — some originate them.

≈

A girl with a future should avoid a man with a past.

≈

Columbus proved that the world is round. What shape is the world in now?

≈

Why is it that when a woman tells a doctor she is all tired out, he immediately looks at her tongue?

≈

What's the best way to force a man to do sit-ups? Put the TV remote control between his toes.

≈

Indifferent people can't build a different world.

≈

A grouch thinks the world is against him — and it is.

≈

It is no longer a question of whether the world is round. These days, the question is how long will it be around?

≈

Nothing is certain in this world except death, taxes and teenagers.

≈

There is not much wrong with the younger generation that becoming a parent and a taxpayer won't cure.

≈

What does a man consider to be a seven-course meal? A hot dog and a six pack.

≈

Women like silent men. They think they are listening.

≈

A chip on the shoulder usually means there's wood higher up.

～

Conversation between Adam and Eve must have been difficult at times because they had no one to talk about.

～

Ole: "Did you fish with flies?"
Sven: "Yes, I fished with them, camped with them, ate with them and slept with them.

～

Harry: "Doctor, how is the man who swallowed the spoon?"
Doctor: "He can hardly stir."

～

Drunk: "Lady, you have two very beautiful legs."
Young lady: "How would you know?"
Drunk: "I counted them."

～

I'm trying to get something for my husband.
Have you had any offers?

～

Harry lost his checkbook in the backyard. It had sprouted a rubber tree.

～

Sheriff: "Do you have any last words before we hang you?"
Prisoner: "I was brought here to be hung, not to make a speech."

～

The paratrooper jumped, counted to ten and pulled the first cord. Nothing happened. He pulled the second cord. Nothing happened. Then he said, "I'll bet that darn truck that was designated to pick me up won't be there either."

～

Man reading Chinese menu: "What is sesame beef ding?"
Waiter: "This dish has beef and sesame seeds."
Man: "What about the ding?"
Waiter: "That's the oven timer."

～

How do you make an elephant fly? First you get a great big zipper.

～

A house is a place to store furniture. A home is a place to store memories.

～

I bought a new showerhead that will save over 7,000 gallons of water per year. Now I'm looking for a place to store all that water.

~

Roland thinks moral fiber is a new breakfast cereal.

~

High taxes have driven me to drink. Now they're taxing beer.

~

Clifford: "My family prays before a meal only when I do the cooking."

~

With all this talk about our bad economy, many are losing the will to live beyond their means.

~

A family budget is a process of checks and balances. The checks wipe out the balances.

~

Larry refused to pay the mechanic for rotating his wheels. "It wasn't needed," he said, "because the wheels on my car rotate every time I drive it."

~

Some people change their mind because it gets dirty.

~

Alex was arrested for feeding a monkey. He was feeding the monkey to the lion.

~

When boys are little, they find boys to play ball. When older, they like girls to play ball.

~

The real reason that mountain climbers tie themselves together is to prevent the sensible one from going home.

~

The teen years are when you know all the answers and nobody asks the questions.

~

Science says millions of germs can live on a single dollar bill for a month. I can't even live a month on a thousand dollars.

~

Judge: "What possible reason could you have for acquitting this murderer?"
Jury: "Temporary insanity."
Judge: "All twelve of you?"

~

Wouldn't it be nice if we could sell our mistakes for what they cost us?

～

Lulu: "I don't know if I have any money left in the bank. I haven't shaken it lately."

～

Sophie: "When I went out with Fred, I had to slap his face five times."
Lulu: "Was he fresh?"
Sophie: "No! I thought he was dead."

～

John: "When is your birthday?"
Erv: "June 5th."
John: "What year?"
Erv: "Every year."

～

There are some people who not only keep you from being lonely, but make you wish you were.

～

There is nothing wrong with the younger generation that the older generation didn't outgrow."

～

Man in a flower shop: "I want something to go with a good alibi."

～

Society is moved forward by men and women of imagination and sustained by those of determination.

～

The cost of living is so high because yesterday's luxuries are now today's necessities.

～

If you want to experience victory, learn to know defeat without losing heart.

～

He is so lazy that if his ship came in, he would expect someone else to unload it for him.

～

If you can keep your head when all about you are losing theirs, then you just don't understand the problem.

～

Keep your eye on the ball, keep your ear to the ground, keep your nose to the grindstone. Now, try and work that way.

～

They call him "garbage man." He has a certain air about him.

~

I loaned a fellow five thousand dollars for plastic surgery. He has not repaid me, and now I don't know what he looks like.

~

Stevie: "What nice thing have you done for an animal?"
Johnny: "Once I kicked a boy for kicking his dog."

~

Snowflakes are one of nature's most fragile things, but just look at what they can do when they stick together.

~

Sophie took Clifford for a ride in her new car. She stopped at a secluded place and took off all her clothing. She said, "Clifford, take what you want." Clifford took the car. When Alex learned about this he exclaimed, "That's good, her clothing wouldn't fit you anyway."

~

Clifford: "The dog ate the meatloaf I made for you."
Sophie: "Stop crying. I'll buy you another dog."

~

A rich uncle's will stated, "And I leave to my beloved nephew all the money he owes me."

~

It's not what you pay a man, but what he costs you that counts. (Will Rogers)

~

Look, I'm not going to engage in a battle of wits with you. I never attack anyone who is unarmed.

~

Clifford: "Please straighten up the house."
Sophie: "Why, is it tilted?"

~

He's driven girls crazy by sending them wires reading: "Ignore first wire."

~

When he goes to the zoo, he needs two tickets — one to get in and one to get out.

~

She has learned that catching a man is like catching a fish. You have to wiggle the bait.

~

Mother to daughter: "When he tells you he wants to be your good friend, make sure he doesn't mean he wants to be good and friendly."

~

As a kid, he played post office. Now he prefers to play pony express because there's more horsing around.

~

There must be a lot of good left in him. None of it ever came out.

~

Lulu: "Doctor, every time Alex drinks tea, he gets a stabbing pain in his right eye."
Doctor: "Tell him to take the spoon out of his cup."

~

On a recent safari, he encountered a bull and a tiger. He shot the tiger first. He figured he could shoot the bull anytime.

~

She gets all her jewelry from a famous millionaire — Woolworth.

~

Do you know the difference between pulling your weight and throwing it around?

~

While courting her, he told her that nothing is good enough for her. It took some time before she learned exactly what he said.

~

When he goes into a cornfield, he scares the crows so badly that the crows bring back the corn they took the year before.

~

Keep smiling. It makes people wonder what you've been up to.

~

He sang a very sad number. In fact, the way he sang, it was pitiful.

~

He thinks he is worth a lot of money just because he has it.

~

I asked a lady not to remove her hat at the movies. It was funnier than the movie.

~

The boss told Lulu, "If your work does not improve, you'll find a pink slip in your envelope. She said, "How nice! Make it a size 32."

~

Alex was sick and needed a doctor's care, but when he arrived at the doctor's office and saw the sign, 9 to 1, he decided to find a doctor who would give him better odds.

~

Beggar: "Can you give me a dollar for a sandwich?"
Alex: "Let's see the sandwich."

~

My friend decided not to have more than four children because he read that every fifth child born is Chinese.

~

When asked for a contribution to help the old ladies home, my question was, "What are the old ladies doing out on a night like this?"

~

Real estate agent: "Would you like to see a model home?"
Clifford: "I sure would. What time does she quit work?"

~

Don't try to judge her by her clothes. There's not enough evidence.

~

He is so lazy he wouldn't even help move his mother-in-law out of the house.

~

Money doesn't grow on trees. Even if it did, he wouldn't shake a limb to get it.

~

He wouldn't join any organization that would take him for a member.

~

He hasn't been himself lately. We hope he'll stay that way.

~

He's been warned that liquor is a slow poison, but he doesn't mind. He's in no hurry.

~

Sophie never really lies about her age. She simply says she's as old as her husband, and then lies about his age.

~

In his footprints on the sands of time, he'll leave only the heel marks.

~

He has more crust than a pie factory.

~

He's out to get you. When he slaps you on the back, it's only to make sure that you'll swallow what he's told you.

~

When you lend him money, he is telling the truth when he says, "I'll be everlastingly indebted to you."

~

He comes from a family of writers. His brother writes novels, his sister writes songs, his mother writes poetry and he writes bum checks.

~

He is managing his life on a cafeteria plan — self-service only.

~

To help a fellow, I lent him some money. Now, it's not only against his principle to pay interest, but also against his interest to pay the principal.

~

My doctor told me to cut down on red meat. I have stopped putting ketchup on my hamburgers.

~

Pregnant executives have it difficult. It's hard to be in management and labor at the same time.

~

Body language is when you have aches and pains and it's because your body is trying to tell you something. As you get older, your body becomes more talkative.

~

Roland: "Why are you dragging the chain?"
Alex: "Did you ever try to push one?"

~

There is something wrong with this health club. The floors are so low, I can't touch my toes.

~

One frog sitting on a lily pad to another: "Time sure is fun when you're having flies."

~

When a strange dog starts sniffing me, I can't tell if he is sniffing me like I'm a cat or like I'm a fire hydrant.

~

Don't be afraid to ask dumb questions. They're easier to handle than dumb mistakes.

~

Doctor: "You are crazy."
Patient: "I want a second opinion."
Doctor: "Very well, you're ugly, too."

~

Man cannot live by bread alone. That's why he gets into jams.

~

Teacher: "How many seconds in a year?"
Alex: "Twelve — January second, February second, March second, etc."

~

The best way to improve your luck is to stop betting.

~

Clifford: "I would like a pork chop, and make it lean."
Waiter: "Lean which way?"

~

Attorney: "If you think your problem is bad now, just wait until we've solved it and you receive the bill."

~

A dry cleaner failed to deliver pants in time for the wedding. The customer sued the cleaning company for "promise of britches."

~

His wife Edith found out that he had a girlfriend named Kate. He should have known that you couldn't have your Kate and Edith too.

~

Principals lose their faculties, teachers lose their class, and accountants lose their balance.

~

A dollar doesn't go as far as it used to, but it sure goes faster.

~

The teacher was explaining to her first-grade class why heat makes objects expand, while cold makes them contract. The teacher asked, "Who can give me an example?" Young Eric said, "In the summertime, the days are long, but in winter they're short."

~

They wanted to put on a Christmas pageant but they couldn't come up with three wise men.

～

No, Lulu. Leisure suits are not cases that lawyers handle in their spare time.

～

One thing common to all success stories is an alarm clock.

～

It's all right to drink like a fish if you drink what a fish drinks.

～

Teacher: "Billy, you missed school yesterday, didn't you?"
Billy: "Not a bit."

～

You can now buy cologne that makes you smell like a cowboy. It's available in a liquid spray or in a semi-solid that you step into.

～

You don't hear the expression soft soap anymore — maybe because soft soap is about one third lye.

～

A sign hanging on the door of a dental office said "Open." Written on the bottom was "wide."

～

"Dad, here's my report card. It's bad again. What do you think it is, heredity or environment?"

～

Ole came home and found Lena naked.
Ole: "Lena, why?"
Lena: "I have nothing to wear."
Ole, opening up the closet: "How about this, or this, or this dress — Hi Sven — or this one?"

～

Wife: "Is it a sin to play golf on Sunday morning?"
Reverend: "The way your husband plays, it's a sin on any day."

～

Teacher: "Jimmy, do you say your prayers before eating?"
Jimmy: "I don't have to, my mother is a good cook."

～

A gossip is a person with a keen sense of rumor.

～

Ole: "My wife Lena will buy anything that's marked down. Last week she purchased an escalator."

~

He: "I'd kiss you but I have scruples."
She: "Oh, that's okay. I've been vaccinated for that."

~

Attorney: "Joe, you really should make out a will."
Joe: "That's probably good advice, but now that I have money, there's no point in dying."

~

Louise: "When are you ever going to get over your procrastination problem?"
Fred: "We'll just have to wait and see."

~

Alex answered the phone: "Sure is," then hung up.
Lulu: "Who was that?"
Alex: "I don't know. Someone just said, 'Long distance from New York.'"

~

Two Norwegians were hunting ducks. At the end of the day, they'd had no luck. Ole turned to Lars and asked, "Do you tink ve maybe haven't been trowing the dog high enough?"

~

Lars had been drinking heavily when he got on an elevator. At the next floor, he was surprised to see a naked woman get on. He took a good long look at her and remarked, "Lady, my wife has an outfit just like that."

~

Clifford: "Lulu looks terrible in that low-cut gown, doesn't she?"
Alex: "As far as I can see, she looks fine."

~

Roland gave his mother-in-law a cemetery plot for her birthday. The next year, he gave her nothing. His wife asked why not. Roland answered, "She didn't use the present I gave her last year."

~

He was in the half that made the top half possible.

~

The only workout some people get is jumping to conclusions, running down their friends, side-stepping their responsibilities and pushing their luck.

~

Ella to a saleswoman at the perfume counter: "Does this perfume really get the results it claims?"
Saleswoman: "If this stuff really worked like that, I wouldn't be standing here eight hours a day."

∾

Little girl telling about Abraham Lincoln: "One night Lincoln drove his Ford to the theater. During the movie, John Wilkes jumped out of the booth and shot Lincoln in his seat."

∾

Lars ate Limburger cheese on Halloween evening and was tipped over four times.

∾

A nurse was asked why she had a rectal thermometer behind her ear. "My goodness, now I remember where I put the ball point pen."

∾

Lena: "Ole, take off my dress."
Ole complied.
Lena: "Now, Ole, take off my stockings; now take off my brassiere and panties."
Again Ole complied.
Lena: "Now, Ole, next time you go into town, you wear your own clothes."

∾

Alex moved to Ireland. He couldn't find a job so he joined the IRA. His first assignment was to blow up a bus. He failed because the tailpipe was too hot.

∾

At some beauty parlors, you get a face full of mud and an earful of dirt.

∾

She's not interested in every Tom, Dick and Harry. She's out to get Jack. He's got plenty of it.

∾

She got tired of trying to get a pearl out of an oyster, so she smartened up and got a diamond out of an old crab.

∾

A man who thinks by the inch and speaks by the yard should be removed by the foot.

∾

The only time in his life that he was ever popular was as a kid in school. He gave all the kids measles just before exams.

∾

She is ready to put her trust in a man if he'll put his money in trust for her.

~

He's tried many diets, but let's face it, he's a poor loser.

~

The hunters shot their bird dog because they could not teach him to fly.

~

A couple at the nudist camp decided to break up because they were seeing too much of each other.

~

Abe Lincoln had a great sense of humor. That's why they put his picture on a penny and called it money.

~

A reporter was sent out on the streets to get man's opinion on modern women. The first man he questioned was 106 years old and said, "I'm afraid I can't be of much help to you, son. You see, I quit thinking about women almost two years ago."

~

Doctor to patient: "You will have to cut down a little on our wonderful American way of life."

~

Mama mosquito said, "If you children are good today, I'll take you to a nudist camp tonight."

~

Son: "Mother, what does fornication mean?"
Mother: "Why don't you ask your father?" (She was not up to explaining that to a five-year-old.)
Son: "Dad, what does fornication mean?"
Dad, hedging the question until he could see that his son was not about to take half an answer: "Son, where did you hear that word?"
Son: "I heard Uncle Sven say, 'fornication like this we should have lutefisk.'"

~

"Yes, the bullet struck my head, went careening into space and . . ."
"How terrible. Did they get it out?"

~

At the Pearly Gates: "How did you get here?"
New arrival: "Flu."

~

Fred: "If a man smashed a clock, could he be accused of killing time?"
Attorney: "Not if he could prove that the clock struck first."

~

One of the outstanding contributions chemistry has made to the world is blondes.

~

Ole's bull was not doing his job. The veterinarian gave Ole a bottle of pills. Sven came over and asked Ole about the medicine for the bull. "What kind of pills are they?" Ole replied, "They're little green pills about the size of a bean. They taste like peppermint."

~

Ole, reading a magazine, remarked, "Lena, do you know every time I breathe, somebody dies?"
Lena: "Why don't you try gargling with some mouthwash?"

~

Ole: "Funny thing about Minnesota. From reading their paper, I found out everyone dies in alphabetical order up here.

~

The best client a lawyer can have is a scared millionaire.

~

Mrs. Smith: "Get up, Del, it's time for school."
Del: "Aw, I don't want to go to school. All the teachers hate me and all the kids say mean things when I try to talk to them."
Mrs. Smith: "But you must go anyway, Del. You're the principal."

~

Son: "Dad, did you see the stork that brought me?"
Dad: "I only saw the bill."

~

Sophie: "Do you wake up grumpy?"
Maggie: "No, I let him sleep."

~

Herb is so bashful he won't open an oyster unless he knocks first.

~

Science has made fantastic strides in the last forty years. It's now only fifty years behind comic books.

~

America is the only country where they lock up the jury and let the prisoners go home.

~

Man: "I want to get a brassiere for my girlfriend."

Saleslady: "What size?"

Man: "Seven-and-a-half."

Saleslady: "You don't understand. Brassieres come in sizes 32-34-36, A, B, C."

Man: "The one I want is size seven-and-a-half!"

Saleslady: "How do you know?"

Man: "I measured."

Saleslady: "How did you measure?"

Man: "With my hat."

～

Two little boys were being pulled in a little red wagon by their dog. In order to make him go, they twisted his tail. A lady stopped to watch. Noticing the manner in which they "motofied" the canine, she said, "My goodness, isn't there some other way you could make your dog go?"

"Yes, ma'am, there is," replied the driver. "We could twist something else, but we use those for passing gear."

～

Boy: "There's nothing I wouldn't do for you."

Girl: "There's nothing I wouldn't do for you."

Girl's hidden little brother: "Gosh, what a revoltin' development. Nobody does nothin' for nobody."

～

While working at a marina, John dropped a forty-pound bag of ice on his foot. John removed his shoe to assess the damage. A passing co-worker glanced at his foot. "Hey, that's real swollen," he exclaimed. "Maybe you should put some ice on it."

～

Priest: "What does a bishop do?"

Young boy: "Moves diagonally."

～

Eric: "I'll answer any question for a hundred dollars."

Dan: "Isn't that a little expensive?"

Eric: "No. Next question."

～

Mabel: "My hobby is whatever interests the man I'm interested in."

～

Sign on a used car: Who will drive this car away for $50? A young man walked into the sales office and pointed to the car. "I'll take a chance. Where's the money?"

～

A Martian landed on earth by accident. He didn't planet that way.

~

Minister announcing the Ladies Aid rummage sale: "This is a good opportunity to get rid of anything that is not worth keeping but is too good to throw away. Don't forget to bring your husbands.

~

Prices on most products are continually going up, but writing paper remains stationary.

~

Dan: "Where did you see that man-eating fish?"
Young Eric: "In a seafood restaurant."

~

Santa has a new reindeer. He is a brown-nosed reindeer. He can run as fast as the others, but can't stop as fast.

~

An astronomer was asked, "How is business?" He answered, "Looking up."

~

Books are made from paper, which comes from trees. That's why we have branch libraries.

~

Lena: "Why are you crying?"
Ole: "My mother just called to tell me that my father died."
Lena (three hours later): "Now what are you crying about?"
Ole: "My brother just called to tell me that his father died too."

~

A doctor, while giving vaccine to the first grader, asked, "Have you ever had measles or chicken pox?"
Child: "No, only corn flakes."

~

Little Johnny had just moved and was not acquainted with his new school. Johnny gave the usual sign to go to the bathroom.
Teacher: "You may go."
Johnny: "I don't know where it is."
Teacher: "When you step out of this door, turn left to the next hall, take a right. It's the first door to the right."
When Johnny returned: "Teacher, I can't find it."
Teacher: "Jimmy, go with Johnny."
Upon their return, Jimmy: "The reason Johnny didn't find it is because his mother put his shorts on backwards."

~

After reading his hometown newspaper, the man telephoned the newspaper editor, identified himself and said, "There is a story about my death in your newspaper."

"I see," said the editor calmly. "And where are you calling from?"

≈

Sophie: "You know, Phil, there's just something about you that attracts women to other men."

≈

Ole died, so Lena went to the local newspaper to place an ad.

Ad salesperson: "What do you want the ad to read?"

Lena: "Ole died."

Salesperson: "What else?"

Lena: "Nothing else, that's enough to pay for."

Salesperson: "Ole lived in the area all his life. I'm sure that people expect more than 'Ole died.' Since you won't spend more for the ad, I'll pay for an extra three words. Now, what will the ad read?"

Lean: "Ole died. Boat for sale."

≈

An old Norwegian male patient asked his nurse for a urinal. The nurse brought a urinal to him. The old man said, "No, no, you don't understand. I want the Milvaukee urinal."

≈

On a recent ocean voyage, a woman fell off the ship into shark-infested water. The sharks looked her over, but promptly swam away. They were man-eating sharks.

≈

Lawyer: "Didn't you say the plaintiff was shot in the woods?"

Doctor: "No, no, in the lumbar region."

≈

During his voyage, Christopher Columbus was the only man in the convoy who was qualified to navigate at night. He therefore slept during the day and was up every night. That was the beginning of the Knights of Columbus.

≈

Mother was busy thumping on the bottom of a catsup bottle when the phone rang. Mother asked Nancy to take the call. "My mother can't come to the phone. She's hitting the bottle."

≈

Emcee introducing the guest speaker: "I won't bore you with all the details. I'll let the speaker do that."

~

Fred saw his new neighbor lady chipping ice, shoveling snow and applying ashes on her driveway. In a friendly manner, Fred asked, "Shouldn't your husband be doing this?"
New neighbor, while sprinkling ashes: "This is my husband."

~

It is all very fine to be able to fly faster than the speed of sound, but what if you want to carry on a conversation?

~

In elementary school I made straight As, but my Bs were a little crooked.

~

Young son: "Mother, how do lions make love?"
Mother: "I don't know. Your dad is a Rotarian."

~

Whenever I see people walking a dog, a question comes to mind. Who is the master? The dog leads the way and the human cleans up after it.

~

If you want to keep your teenager out of hot water, put some dirty dishes in the water.

~

Two fellows having coffee — First fellow to waitress: "I'll have a cup of coffee."
Second fellow: "I'll also have a cup of coffee, and be sure to put it in a clean cup."
Waitress returning with two cups of coffee: "Which one of you fellows wanted the clean cup?"

~

There are too many people in too many cars in too much of a hurry going too many directions to get nowhere for nothing.

~

Hunter: "I'm giving up my sport of hunting elephants. The decoys are just too heavy for a guy my age."

~

Mother: "Billy, I told you to let your little brother play with the sled one half of the time."
Billy: "That's what I've been doing. I take the sled down the hill and I let him take it up."

~

Sam to his younger brother: "I bet you can't climb this beam."
Tommy: "I'm not that stupid. I'd get halfways up and you'd turn off the flashlight."

～

Teaching may not be the best paying job, but it is a job with class.

～

Some reading may be dull, but cookbooks are full of stirring passages.

～

Golf used to be a rich man's sport. Now it has millions of poor players.

～

A horseshoe is a symbol of good luck, particularly if it's on the right horse.

～

Behind every successful antique shop is a junk store.

～

Many start out to set the world on fire and end up settling for a back-yard barbecue.

～

Crime doesn't pay, but it does provide free room and board if you're caught.

～

Modern movies contain so much bad language you'd think they were being made by a bunch of irate golfers.

～

You won't be a live wire if you touch one.

～

Studies show that most docks collapse because of pier pressure.

～

While many argue whether we came from apes, most people agree that we're going to the dogs.

～

Scientists have discovered that the only thing fireproof is the boss's son.

～

There are many things you can do to live longer, and if you don't live longer, it will seem longer.

～

Thanksgiving is a day on which all people are thankful they're not turkeys.

∼

Sign in a restaurant: Eat now, pay waiter.

∼

You don't really know someone until you walk a mile in their shoes, and by then you're too far away to get acquainted.

∼

The reason some folks don't show more horse sense is that they don't want to be saddled with responsibility.

∼

Sailors to two girls walking home: "Where are you going?"
Girls: "We're walking home."
Sailors: "It's too early to go home."
Girls: "No, it's not too early. We're out after hours."
Sailors: "That's good. We're out after ours, also."

∼

Lena requested a potholder as a Christmas gift. Ole bought a girdle for her.

∼

An inexperienced speaker arose in confusion after dinner and stammered slowly, "M-m-my friends, when I came here tonight, only God and myself knew what I was going to say to you, and now only God knows."

∼

A proud father, after seeing his son's report card, remarked, "No doubt about it. This kid inherited my intelligence." His mother replied softly, "That's very true. But I kept mine."

∼

Lena wanted something real snappy for her birthday. Ole bought her a mousetrap.

∼

Ann: "At your age, how do you do it?"
Fred: "What makes you think I still do it?"

∼

This is not dirty talk. It's how you read and comprehend it.

∼

Patient to psychiatrist: "I keep feeling as if I was covered all over with gold paint."
Psychiatrist: "That's probably just a gilt complex."

~

Fire inspector: "What happened?"
Roland: "When I came home with my friend, I opened the door and smelled gas. Then my friend lit a match to see."
Fire inspector: "A match? But that's the last thing you do."
Roland: "Yes, it was the last thing my friend did."

~

A professional boxer will tell you that it's better to give than to receive.

~

He claims he's a self-made man. At least he's willing to take the blame.

~

Communism bothers me. They have nothing and want to share it with us.

~

The psychiatrist charged him a double fee because he had a split personality.

~

Lord help me to do with a smile those things I must do anyway.

~

One form of loneliness is to have a memory and no one to share it with.

~

There are times when a quiet listener outshines a brilliant conversationalist.

~

Be careful if you stretch the truth. It may snap back.

~

Lars: "I wish I had enough money to buy an elephant."
Ole: "Why do you want an elephant?"
Lars: "I don't want an elephant, I merely wish I had that much money."

~

Diner: "Are you sure you're the waiter I gave my order to?"
Waiter: "What makes you ask?"
Diner: "By now, I expected a much older man."

~

Mother: "Why did you kick your little brother in the stomach?"
Boy: "Because he turned around."

~

She was taken in by a girdle.

～

Children have become so expensive that only the poor can afford them.

～

Lena has a sobering effect on Ole. She hides his bottle.

～

Jeff: "I was thinking of you yesterday when I was cleaning out the stable."

～

Two fellows were driving down the street. The driver continued to run red lights. The passenger asked, "Why are you running all the red lights?"
Driver: "Because my brother does."
When they arrived at the next set of signals, the light was green, but the driver made a full stop. The passenger asked, "Why do you stop for a green light?"
Driver: "Because my brother might be coming through."

～

I saw a sign that read fine for parking, so I did.

～

This is a tough neighborhood. Any cat here with a tail is a tourist.

～

They were lying in bed together — she was lying to him and he was lying to her.

～

A girl that is free for the evening can be expensive.

～

Alex: "I've lost my luggage."

Harry: "How did that happen?"
Alex: "The cork fell off."

～

A young lady passenger asked the pilot, "How do you manage to fly this plane in the dark?"
Pilot: "There's a light on the tip of the right wing and a light on the tip of the left wing, and another light on the tail. All I have to do is keep the plane between the lights.

～

A city fellow crossing a farmer's field said to the farmer, "Is this bull safe?" The farmer said, "He's a lot safer than you are."

～

George: "My doctor tells me I can't play golf."
Jim: "So he's played with you also?"

~

Gary: "How long are you in jail for, Roland?"
Roland: "Two weeks."
Gary: "What's the charge?"
Roland: "No charge. Everything is free."
Gary: "I mean, what did you do?"
Roland: "Oh, I shot my wife."
Gary: "You killed your wife and you're in jail for only two weeks?"
Roland: "That's all — then I get hanged."

~

I read that a fellow invented a game which in some ways resembles golf. That's the game I've been playing.

~

Clifford, hiring a caddy: "Can you count, young man?"
Boy: "Yes, sir."
Clifford: "How many are four and five and three?"
Boy: "Nine, sir."
Clifford: "You'll do just fine."

~

Al Capone: "You can get more done with a kind word and a gun than you can with just a kind word."

~

CPAs watch their figures.

~

Waitress: "What would you like?"
Customer: "I originally came in for breakfast, but if lunch is ready now, I'll have supper."

~

Golf pro: "Tee the ball."
Roland: "Sure I see the ball, but why the baby talk?"

~

Wesley: "I hear you're not going to Germany this year."
Wally: "No, it's England we're not going to this year. It was Germany we didn't go to last year."

~

A man walked up to the reception desk at the hotel and said to the receptionist, "May I have some writing paper and envelopes bearing the name of this hotel?"
Receptionist: "Are you a guest at this hotel?"
Customer: "No, young lady, I'm not a guest. I'm paying $140 a day."

~

A sure way to become a millionaire playing the horses is to start with two million.

~

Ole and Lena were driving forty miles an hour over the speed limit. The highway patrol pulled them over.

Officer: "I'll have to give you a speeding ticket."

Ole: "If you do, I'll see to it that you lose your job — and I'll push your nose down to your belly button."

Officer to Lena: "Does he always talk like that?"

Lena: "No, only when he's drunk."

≈

People who cut too many corners may end up going around in circles.

≈

The reason we do so much better in the Olympics than Mexico is that everyone who can run, jump or swim fast is already in the United States.

≈

Hospitals take X-rated pictures.

≈

Lulu wanted to stay young so she decided to use that oil of delay stuff.

≈

Boy to father: "I did what George Washington did — I went down in history."

≈

He's not open-minded — he has holes in his head.

≈

I was going to buy you a handkerchief but I didn't know the size of your nose.

≈

Clifford: "Why do you dress so sharp lately? You seem to be in the latest fashions. That's not like you."

Alex: "My doctor told me I'm impotent. When you're impotent, you should look impotent."

≈

Murphy: "I saw in the paper that you advertised for a wife."

Casey: "That I did."

Murphy: "Any replies?"

Casey: "Yes, several. They all offered me their wives."

≈

Now that I can afford to lose a golf ball, I can't hit it that far.

≈

Do some down-to-earth work. Plant a garden.

≈

Thank you for the eggnog and thank you for the spirit in which it was served.

~

The lessons I learned across my father's knee sure made me smart.

~

He's not a liar. He merely lives on the wrong side of the facts.

~

A neighborhood bar is where a body meets a body coming in for rye.

~

Customer when the waitress brought a piece of pie: "There should be a minimum wedge law."

~

If you order soft drinks, you have no kick coming.

~

He is living proof that a woman can take a joke.

~

United States women buy 498,000 girdles, and they have the figures to prove it.

~

Cheer up. Birds also have bills, yet they sing.

~

Alex: "Are you going to see more of her?"
Harry: "There really isn't much more to see."

~

Harry: "Do you believe in the here-after?"
Larry: "I sure do. That's what I'm here after."

~

Ole was hired as a watchman for a local hotel beach area. One day Ole noticed a shapely young lady sun-bathing without any clothes. "Lady," said Ole, "you can't do dat out here in public."
"I have a divine right," murmured the young beauty.
"Ya, I know," said Ole, "and the left vun ain't so bad either."

~

Sophie and Clifford had to sell their waterbed. They were drifting apart.

~

If my salespeople would be self-starters, I wouldn't have to be a crank.

~

Lost items are always found in the last place you look.

∼

The reason love is so intoxicating is because it's generally made in the still of the night.

∼

Some girls think good housekeeping is a magazine.

∼

Your bank balance gets shot when you are too quick on the draw.

∼

He had to give up his career because of fallen arches. He was an architect.

∼

Clifford: "You're a doll."
Sophie: "I don't like that a bit. A doll is a stuffed dummy."

∼

I heard they found Hoffa in the yellow pages under concrete.

∼

After you eat at some of those places, you need an after-dinner mint — a mint like they have in Denver.

∼

New Year's Eve is when more people get loaded than trucks.

∼

With the present medical costs, no one will die laughing.

∼

She has just been recalled by her beauty parlor.

∼

New Yorker and a Texan looking at Niagara Falls: "I bet they don't have anything like this in Texas."
Texan: "No, but in Texas we have plumbers that could fix it."

∼

"I'm sorry," said the dentist. "I can't see you today. I have eighteen cavities to fill," and he picked up his golf clubs and went out the back door.

∼

Dolphins are so intelligent that within a few weeks after captivity, they can train a man to stand on the very edge of the pool and throw them food three times a day.

∼

It's no use asking you to act like a human being — you don't do imitations.

~

Gambling away the rent money is a moving experience.

~

When they told me they wanted an emcee of a certain caliber, I was delighted. After looking up the word "caliber" in the dictionary, to my horror it read, "Caliber: something to do with the size of a bore."

~

Kirsten had a kitten, Eric had a pup, and Kevin has a crocodile who ate the others up.

~

When you're in deep water, it's a good idea to keep your mouth shut.

~

In one year, millions of electric drills are sold, not because people want electric drills. What some people want are the holes. The service those drills render is what makes them so important and valuable. What about people?

~

On Thanksgiving Day, most people are bird watchers.

~

When I took my young grandson who is learning to read to the store, he picked up a package of pantyhose from my cart. "Q-U-E-E-N-S-I-Z-E," he read aloud. Then he looked at me. "Why, Grandma," he said, to the amazement of everyone nearby, "you're the same size as our mattress."

~

Clifford: "We are having six gobblers for Thanksgiving dinner. They're all relatives."

~

The earth is overpopulated because when God said to go and replenish the earth, He thought we'd be as lazy about that as we are about everything else.

~

How many miles can you get from a bale of hay?

~

Common sense is not as common as it used to be.

~

If what you don't know won't hurt you is true, then a lot of folks ain't hurting much.

~

Just because a man looks at a pretty girl twice is no sign of poor vision.

∼

Teacher: "I want to talk to you about your little boy."
Mother: "Nothing doing. I had him all summer and not once did I call you."

∼

Neighbor: "Are you a good boy?"
Boy: "No, ma'am, I'm the kind of boy my mother won't let me play with."

∼

Ida: "Is your water supply healthy?"
Tina: "It certainly is. We use only well water."

∼

My brother and sister-in-law often give me shave lotion and cologne. I think they like me okay, but they just don't like the way I smell.

∼

An undertaker is the last person to let you down.

∼

She called them slacks but there wasn't a bit of slack in them.

∼

The reason little pigs leave home is because their dad is a big boar.

∼

He sells cockleburs to tourists as porcupine eggs.

∼

If you wish to be well-healed, stay on your toes.

∼

He is a hundred percent right two percent of the time.

∼

You get virgin wool from ugly sheep and from sheep that run the fastest.

∼

Short skirts are responsible for high interest.

∼

I don't drink anymore. I don't drink any less, either.

∼

Roland wanted to make some strong beer out of kangaroo hops.

∼

Alex bought a fifth on the third for the Fourth.

~

Lena wanted to be a bubble dancer. Her father said, "No soap."

~

A woman who had thirteen children ran out of names (to call her husband).

~

"There are things in life bigger than money," says Sophie.
Clifford: "Yes, bills."

~

I don't want to be a king. I would just like to live like one.

~

He said he got into trouble seeing a fire. Actually, he got into trouble seeing an old flame.

~

A well-reared girl should not wear slacks.

~

Sven: "Can you concentrate on two things at one time?"
Ole: "Yes, a sweater girl."

~

He lost control of his car. He failed to make the payments.

~

That girl wears a formal gown and can be seen in the best places.

~

We saw a girlie show yesterday. I saw so much navel movement, I thought the United States fleet was in.

~

Lars: "That Clifford is a regular guy."
Sven: "Yes, he must eat bran flakes every day."

~

Doctor: "Drink lots of water. Frequent drinking of water prevents you from becoming stiff at the joints."
Gus: "Yes, but some joints don't serve water."

~

My financial problems are simple. I'm merely short of money.

~

Roland got his deer and was pulling it toward camp by the tail.

~

Alex: "Wouldn't it be much easier to pull him head first?"
Roland: "Maybe so, but I'm not going that way."

~

My friend went to school to learn how to read and riot.

~

He rode tall in his saddle until his blisters broke.

~

Most flies near a house go for a screen test.

~

Gus: "These bath salts taste okay, but I don't think you get the same results as you do from taking a bath."

~

Joe doesn't exaggerate, he just remembers big.

~

There are days when we wish newscasters would cast their news somewhere else.

~

Women are tricky. They use sugar and spice to cover the ice.

~

Some folks love their country for the same reason that the farmer loves his cow — because he could milk it.

~

Ole: "I can't see what keeps those girls from freezing."
Lena: "You're not supposed to."

~

History may yet record that liberty was ushered in by a cracked bell and tossed out by crackpots.

~

You have a problem when your dentist says you need a bridge and you don't have the money to pay the toll.

~

Gus says if the news media didn't glamorize demonstrators, protestors, hijackers, etc., we wouldn't have so many of them.

~

My uncle thought that families with properly spaced children would be best spaced about one hundred yards apart.

~

A Texas court ruled that when a woman hits a man, it is simple assault. When a man hits a woman, it is aggravated assault. And, boy, can women be aggravating.

~

His two loose teeth were attributed to one loose tongue.

~

Al says he's not spoiled — it's just the shave lotion he uses.

~

These cigarette girls must be expecting a mild winter.

~

Ole: "The other day Lena said that I was perfect."
Sven: "Which day was that?"
Ole: "That's the same day she called me an idiot."

~

Ole: "What caused this population explosion?"
Sven: "Matches."

~

A burp gun is not used on babies.

~

Some people confine their exercise to jumping to conclusions, running up bills, stretching the truth, bending over backward, lying down on the job, sidestepping responsibilities, pushing their luck, keeping their chin up, and sticking their neck out.

~

Stopping at third base adds no more to the score than striking out.

~

Faith, hope and charity — if we had more of the first two, we would need much less of the last one.

~

You need a raft of money to keep the family afloat these days.

~

Some families can track their ancestry back three hundred years, but can't tell you where their children were last night.

~

A fool and his money are soon parted. The rest of us wait until income tax time.

~

When you bury the hatchet, don't bury it in your enemy's back.

~

Sophie: "Do you love me still?"
Clifford: "Yes, better than any other way."

~

Most of us like a person who comes right out and says what he thinks, especially when he thinks like we do.

~

You can say what you please in America, but nobody listens.

~

Many who howl loudest about free speech have nothing worth saying.

~

Christmas is a time when people want their past forgotten and their present remembered.

~

Most girls prefer to be looked over rather than overlooked.

~

Some girls think it's better to be well formed than well informed.

~

Many a girl is looking for a man with a strong will — made out to her.

~

Most people aim to do right but are merely poor shots. First you must know where the goal is.

~

Since three-fourths of the earth's surface is water and one-fourth is land, it's very clear that God intended us to spend three-fourths of our time fishing and one-fourth plowing.

~

At last count, gossip was running down more people than automobiles.

~

Idle gossip keeps some folks busy.

~

A man who is always losing his head probably has a screw loose.

~

When you get to heaven, you may be surprised to see some of the people there. Many may be just as surprised to see you.

~

The reason history repeats itself is that most people were not listening the first time.

~

The best acting job is done by the man congratulating his ex-wife's husband on the choice he made.

~

The warmth of a home is not necessarily determined by the insulation, windows or heating system. It takes love to warm a home.

~

Why is it when you go to a hotel for a change and rest, the bellboy gets the change and the hotel gets the rest?

~

Lots of people play dumb. Unfortunately, many are not playing.

~

The only thing he does on time is buy.

~

People that smoke and drink commit suicide on the installment plan.

~

Not all educated people are intelligent.

~

A juvenile delinquent sows his wild oats, and his parents pray for a crop failure.

~

Education should include knowledge of what to do with it.

~

In Las Vegas, you can't beat the climate, sunshine or the slot machines.

~

Not all the teeth put into our laws these days are wisdom teeth.

~

Old lawyers never die. They just lose their appeal.

~

A critically ill lawyer was leafing through the Bible looking for loopholes.

~

The nice thing about spring fever is that it makes laziness respectable.

~

How can shiftless people get into high gear?

~

It's what we learn after we know it all that really counts.

~

You should not pull the wool over people's eyes. They may recognize the yarn.

~

The only thing that went off as planned was my alarm clock.

~

Many people think life would be so much more enjoyable if we didn't have to work our way through it.

~

Roland says: "Folks who think they know it all are amusing to us folks who do."

~

The world needs more warm hearts and fewer hotheads.

~

A budding love these days is a blooming experience.

~

A young lady concluded her prayer with this appeal: "Lord, I would appreciate it very much if you would send my mother a nice son-in-law."

~

The average man is forty-two around the chest, forty-four around the waist, ninety-six around the golf course and a nuisance around the house.

~

A tip to the young male driver — forget the girl and hug the road.

~

Teenage boys who whistle at girls are merely going through a stage that will probably pass in sixty years.

~

Even if a man could understand women, he still wouldn't believe it.

~

A man must be big enough to admit his mistakes, smart enough to profit from them and strong enough to correct them.

~

The most necessary automobile accessory is a wallet.

~

This country has turned out some great men in the past. Then there are some others that are not so great that ought to be turned out.

～

Most people like change that jingles in their pocket.

～

Crime costs billions, and we are certainly getting our money's worth.

～

It seems men are born to be collectors. First they collect bugs, toads, and marbles; then they collect girls, kisses and ties; then money, worries and a family; then golf trophies, dirty jokes and hair tonics; and finally, they collect pains, symptoms and memories.

～

Opera is where a guy gets stabbed in the back and, instead of bleeding, he sings.

～

Many a violin sounds as though its strings are still in the cat.

～

Money is a pretty good temporary cure for poverty.

～

Money is an excellent gift. Everything else is too expensive.

～

I wouldn't need money if other people weren't so crazy about it. That's why money gets out of hand so quickly.

～

It's difficult to save money when your neighbors keep buying things you can't afford.

～

It's sad to see people squandering money when you know you can't help them.

～

The way many Americans pass the buck, it's no wonder the dollar bill wears out.

～

Santa Claus is not the only one in the red.

～

A mother takes twenty-one years to make a man of her boy, then another woman comes along and makes a fool of him in twenty minutes.

～

You can tell it's an old movie when the doctor tells the patient, "You're as sound as a dollar."

∼

The most difficult thing to open is a closed mind.

∼

Don't be so narrow-minded that your ears rub together.

∼

Mother Nature makes blunders too. She often gives the biggest mouths to those who have the least to say.

∼

The difference between a luxury and a necessity depends on whether your neighbor has it and you don't.

∼

Many are for justice that brings them rewards and gives others what they have coming to them.

∼

If you have an unpleasant neighbor, chances are that he does too.

∼

May your troubles in the coming year be as short-lived as your resolutions.

∼

The agriculture department says the average American consumes 1,148 pounds of food each year. A lot of it goes to waist.

∼

If he were a truck, he would be required to have a wide load sign.

∼

Nurse: "Why don't you eat your Jell-O?"
Old man: "I'm not going to eat anything that's more nervous than I am."

∼

Going to eternal rest doesn't mean landing a job with the government.

∼

Every child comes into the world endowed with liberty, opportunity and a share of the war debt.

∼

You cannot unsnarl a traffic jam by blowing horns.

∼

Doctor to patient: "Of course you're furious over the price of your medication. That's one of the side effects."

~

A college education is very educational. It teaches the student's parents how to do without a lot of things.

~

A deer hunter, while sitting in his blind mounted to a tree fifteen feet off the ground, saw a buck coming. He took a shot, then he took another shot, and by the time he put the bottle down, the deer was gone.

~

A deer hunter got his deer okay, but he didn't know what to do with the saddle.

~

The trouble with the average juvenile delinquent is not always apparent. Sometimes it's both parents.

~

There are three major parties — republican, democrat, and cocktail.

~

Keeping peace in the family requires patience, love, understanding and at least two television sets.

~

Some motorists keep pedestrians in good running conditions. Even if a pedestrian is wrong, he doesn't deserve the death penalty.

~

Some people don't get ulcers — they're only carriers.

~

Both a preacher and a real estate salesman will tell you that there is a better place for you to be.

~

We try to teach our children good manners. One day I set a glass of juice in front of my two-year-old and asked her, "What do you say?" She looked at me, then smiled, lifted her glass and said, "Cheers."

~

Penicillin is a wonder drug because any time your doctor wonders what you have, that's what you get.

~

Most American doctors do not believe in acupuncture. They would rather stick us with their bills.

~

Doctor: "I'm afraid you are beyond medical help — you have a cold."

~

As long as there are final exam-
inations in school, there will be
prayers in school.

~

Some men fight for principles,
others defend prejudices.

~

Our problems have become so
complex that even taxi drivers and
teenagers don't have the answers.

~

Schoolteachers have to face their
problems every day; bus drivers have
their problems behind them.

~

Bartender: "Feel free to discuss your
problems here, but be sure you
don't create any.

~

Many people have too much month
left at the end of their money.

~

A diet is what you keep putting off
while you keep putting on.

~

Progress is wonderful. Seventy-five
years ago, only hobos cooked their
food outside, and now many of us
do.

~

Progress is due to those who were
not satisfied to let well enough
alone. If only we could have made
as much progress with people as
we have made with things.

~

Many people can't stand prosperity,
but most people don't have to.

~

A psychiatrist's couch is where you
land when you're off your rocker.

~

A new branch of psychiatry has been
started — psycho ceramics. It's the
study of crackpots.

~

Psychologists say that no one should
try to keep too much to themselves.
The IRS is of the same opinion.

~

Introduction: "We're very pleased
to have as our guest speaker a man
who has to catch his plane in twenty
minutes."

~

Anybody who thinks he knows all the answers isn't up to date on the questions.

~

Sometimes you can dodge a question with a long-winded answer.

~

A speaker who doesn't strike oil in twenty minutes should stop boring.

~

There are two kinds of speakers. One needs no introduction and the other deserves none.

~

What the speaker won't boil down, the audience must sweat out.

~

Speaker: "I understand my job is to speak to you. Your job is to listen. I hope I finish before you do."

~

Speaker: "Before I start my speech, I would like to say something."

~

Henry not only dines with the upper set, he uses his lowers too.

~

She drinks cocktails and has a millionaire for a chaser.

~

Waitress: "How would you like your eggs served?"
Roland: "On a thick slice of ham."

~

Note to teacher: "Please excuse Jimmy for being absent. He had a new baby brother. It was not his fault."

~

Roland said, "Don't abuse the privilege of being stupid."

~

Maggie: "Haven't I always been fair to you?"
Harry: "Yes, but I want you to be fair and warmer."

~

Jim: "What's the best thing for hives?"
Sam: "Bees."

~

Harry: "Who was sorry when the prodigal son returned?"
Fred: "The fatted calf."

~

Newsboy: "Extra, extra, read all about it — two men swindled."
Customer: "Say, there isn't anything in here about two men being swindled."
Newsboy: "Extra, extra, three men swindled."

~

A sign on a butcher shop in London proclaims proudly: "We make sausage for the Queen." On the other side of the street another butcher shop displays a sign: "God save the Queen."

~

"Please send me eighty-five dollars for toilet articles and stuff," wrote a soldier from Russia to his wife. "Enclosed is five dollars for toilet articles," answered his wife. "Your stuff is over here."

~

Doctor: "You must avoid all forms of excitement."
Patient: "Can I look at them on the street?"

~

Mary had a little dress, dainty, chic and airy. It didn't show the dirt a bit, but gosh, how it showed Mary.

~

Jack: "Have you noticed that most successful men are bald?"
Fred: "Naturally, they come out on top."

~

No matter how low a man gets, there is always a woman and a dog that will love him.

~

Wife: "How many fish was it you caught on Saturday, Harry?"
Harry: "Six, honey — all beauties."
Wife: "I thought so. That fish shop has made a mistake again. They charged us for eight."

~

Women understand women. That's why they like men better.

~

Joe: "What are you planting?"
Moe: "A dogwood tree."
Joe: "Gonna grow some pups?"
Moe: "No, I just like its bark."

~

Landlady: "I thought I saw you taking a gentleman up to your apartment last night."
Tenant: "That's what I thought too."

~

Doctor: "Have you kept a chart on his progress?"
Nurse: "No, but I can show you my diary."

~

Classified ad: "If the person who stole the jar of alcohol from the basement will return grandma's appendix, no questions will be asked."

~

Lady on phone: "Are you Harry?"
Man: "Not especially, lady. But I'm a long way from bald."

~

The maid treated her boyfriend like dirt. She hid him under her bed.

~

Roland made a monkey out of himself by reaching for the wrong limb.

~

Flattery is a perfume to be smelled, not swallowed.

~

For sale: "Mattress and large diamond engagement ring, used only a few weeks."

~

Ole: "Are you free tonight?"
Maggie: "Not exactly free, but not really expensive."

~

Sir: "My secretary, being a lady, will not type what I think of you. Because I am a gentleman, I won't dictate it. You, being neither, will understand what I mean."

~

Old lady to bus driver: "Must you stop at every telephone pole?"
Bus Driver: "Sorry, lady, this is a Greyhound."

~

She has put on the dog for so long that now she's gone to chasing cars.

~

"I might as well put the motion before the house," said the chorus girl as she danced out onto the stage.

~

A bank is an institution where you can borrow money if you present sufficient evidence that you don't really need it.

~

He: "Thank you for the dance."
She: "The pressure was all mine."

∼

Lulu: "Just think, Roland, we don't have to pull down the shades. We're married now."

∼

Young Mother Hubbard went to the cupboard to get the iceman a bracer; but hubby came in and instead of the gin, the iceman got only the chaser.

∼

Recruiting officer: "I suppose you want a commission."
Recruit: "No, thanks. I'm such a poor shot that I'd rather work on a straight salary."

∼

Eric giggled when the teacher read the story of a man who swam the river three times before breakfast.
Teacher: "Eric, do you doubt that a strong swimmer could do that?"
Eric: "I don't question the man doing that, but I wonder why he didn't make it four times and get back to the side where his clothes were."

∼

George didn't know she was a golfer when she asked him to play a round.

∼

Many a youth is burning the midnight oil in order to keep some flaming beauty from going out on him.

∼

If you knew Suzie like I know Suzie, her old man would be after you with a shotgun, too.

∼

Telegram to army major overseas: "Baby arrived. Features yours; fixtures mine."

∼

Colonel: "You say you served with the army in France?"
Cook: Yes, Sir. Officer's cook for two years and wounded twice."
Colonel: "You're lucky. It's a wonder they didn't kill you."

∼

A circus elephant came loose one night and found its way into an old lady's garden. The old lady called the police saying, "There is a huge animal in my garden and he's pulling up my cabbage with his tail."
Officer: "What's he doing with the cabbage?"
Old lady: "You wouldn't believe me if I told you."

∼

First lawyer to his opponent: "You're a cheat."
Second lawyer: "You're a liar."
Judge: "Now that the attorneys have identified each other, shall we proceed with the case?"

~

"My success is positively assured," said the recent purchaser of a new dairy farm. "It's in the bag."

~

Ernest: "Did you ever see anything like you saw at that show last evening?"
Roland: "Not since I was weaned."

~

Lester: "I saw a baby today that gained ten pounds in two weeks on elephant's milk."
Ernest: "Whose baby was it?"
Lester: "The elephant's."

~

When the traffic cop asked her why she didn't have a red light on her car, Dora answered angrily that it wasn't that kind of car, and besides, she wasn't that kind of girl.

~

The other day I saw a magician walk down the street and turn into a grocery store.

~

Junior: "Daddy, what's a sweater girl?"
Daddy: "A girl who works in a sweater factory. (Slight pause.) Where did you get that question?"
Junior: "Never mind that, Daddy, where did you get that answer?"

~

The admiral's daughter exclaimed, "Golly, I'm tired and absolutely famished! I haven't had a bite to eat all day."
Admiral: "Where were you all day? Why haven't you eaten? I distinctly remember telling you that it was arranged for you to mess with the officers."
Daughter: "Yes, Daddy, and I want to have a talk with you about that. That's the reason I didn't get to eat."

~

Little boy at the beach: "Daddy, why do pretty girls wear their water wings all the time?"

~

Sophie: "When you stay after class with the professor, what do you do? Study history?"
Lulu: "No, make it."

~

Here is a gift that your ancestors were very fond of — a coconut and bananas.

~

It cost him five hundred dollars to trace his ancestors, and a thousand to keep it quiet.

~

Unlicensed Gus stopped doing electrical work on a major project. He didn't want to get caught in a union suit.

~

Army barber: "Do you want to keep your sideburns?"
Recruit: "I sure do."
Barber: "Did you bring a container for them?"

~

Lulu considered going into the movies, but she was the only one who considered it. However, she has appeared in shorts.

~

Clifford: "I sure like you in that formal dress."
Southern girl: "Sho' nuff?"
Clifford: "It sure does."

~

Figuring out your income tax is a lesson in addition, subtraction and extraction.

~

Golfer: "How would you have played that last shot?"
Caddy: "Under an assumed name, sir."

~

Students shall not be awarded letters for participating in sports until they can tell which letter it is.

~

Sign on the back of an electrician's truck: "If you can't find your shorts, call us."

~

The difference between a cute little child and a budding delinquent is whether or not he's yours.

~

She was only a garbage collector's daughter, but she was nothing to be sniffed at.

~

Dora is fond of clothes, although she is not entirely wrapped up in them.

~

Accidents happen every hunting season because both the gun and hunter are loaded.

~

It's not the fall that hurts; it's the sudden stop.

~

Many think that skiing is a winter activity. For me, it's a fall sport.

~

A lawyer driving in Chicago hit a guy and knocked him nine feet off the road, then sued him for leaving the scene of the accident.

~

It's a small world once you've made the long trip to the airport.

~

You shouldn't get angry at someone who knows more than you do. After all, it's not his fault.

~

Automobiles wouldn't be so dangerous if the horsepower of the engine was in direct proportion to the horse sense of the driver.

~

Nature gave me two ends — one to sit on and one to think with. Success or failure depends on the one used the most.

~

Lulu: "I need a spicy book to read." Roland: "Here's a Mexican cookbook."

~

There is a new baby food on the market. It's half orange juice and half garlic. It makes the baby healthier and easier to find in the dark.

~

Nothing changes a small boy's appearance like a bar of soap.

~

If a person has no education, he's forced to use his brains.

~

Your brain becomes a mind when it is fortified with knowledge.

~

Some people have more money than brains, but not for long.

~

A girdle is a garment to hold a woman in when she goes out.

~

The new bikinis make women look better, and make men look better also.

~

The nice thing about money is that it never clashes with anything you're wearing.

~

To err is human. To really louse it up takes a computer.

~

Eggheads and boneheads get equal billing at the cemetery.

~

The world's most conceited man celebrated his own birthday by sending his mother a telegram of congratulations.

~

The most irritating person at a class reunion is the guy who has all his hair and has money.

~

Lena: "Our little Ole is going to be an astronaut."
Ole: "What makes you think that?"
Lena: "I called the school and asked about him. His teacher said he is taking up space."

~

Bakery Sign: Cakes 66¢; Upside down cakes 99¢.

~

The food prices at some places are so high that men who go bankrupt blame it on the food they ate.

~

Why do they call it a freeway? Don't they realize what it costs to operate a vehicle?

~

Business is tough these days. If a man does something wrong, he gets fined. If he does something right, he gets fined.

~

For sale: Antique desk suitable for lady with thick legs and large drawers.

~

Get rid of your duties — discharge them.

∼

Sven: "Doctor, can you give me something for my wind?"
Doctor: "Here's a kite."

∼

Customer: "Can you clean these pants?"
Dry cleaner: "Well, ma'am, these pants are satin."
Customer: "I know that! I want you to remove whatever it was I sat in."

∼

Some women diet to keep their girlish figure; others to keep their boyish husband.

∼

I'm on a seafood diet. Whenever I see food, I eat it.

∼

Teacher: "How do you keep milk from getting sour?"
Little Ole: "Leave it in the cow."

∼

Sven: "Ole, did you have an accident."
Ole: "No, I was tossed by a bull, but it was no accident. He did it on purpose."

∼

Grandma to granddaughter when leaving: "Come again soon. We'd like to see more of you."
Granddaughter: "But there isn't any more of me."

∼

Teacher: "If I lay three eggs here and five eggs there, how many eggs will I have?"
Little Eric: "I don't believe you can do it."

∼

Roland: "Lulu, it's your son who believes in free speech. He's calling collect again."

∼

Tourist: "Excuse me, can you tell me where this road goes to?"
Old man: "It don't go nowhere. It's been here as long as I have."

∼

Tourist: "What time is it?"
Village boy: "It's twelve o'clock."
Tourist: "I thought it was much later than that."
Village boy: "Oh, no, it never gets later than that in these parts."
Tourist: "How's that?"
Village boy: "Well, after twelve o'clock, it goes back to one."

∼

Little Ole: "Mom, there's a man at the door collecting for the old folk's home. Shall I give him Grandpa?"

~

Dad: "Son, please get me a screwdriver."
Son: "Sorry, Dad, I've got the orange juice but I can't find the vodka."

~

She was looking for a great vacation, and he was the last resort.

~

Teacher: "Name a country that's cold."
Little Ole: "Chile."

~

Teacher: "Eric, you have drawn that horse very nicely, but where is the cart?"
Eric: "The horse will draw that."

~

Teacher: "Write the longest sentence you can compose."
Little Ole: "Life imprisonment."

~

He is not entirely useless; he can serve as a horrible example.

~

A mother heard her son use a number of words and phrases that were objectionable and said, "From whom did you get those words?"
Young boy: "From Shakespeare."
Mother: "Well, don't ever play with him again."

~

Sophie: "Is your husband a bookworm?"
Lulu: "Oh, no, just an ordinary one."

~

A college education benefits the person most who is willing to learn after he receives it.

~

Being able to profit from the mistakes of others is the least expensive education you can get.

~

Love your enemies and they will wonder what kind of deal you are trying to pull. It'll drive them nuts.

~

Don't mind the fellow who belittles you. He is merely trying to cut you down to his size.

~

Young man: "Er ... sir, I ... er, I mean, I came to say that your daughter tells me she ... er ... loves me."
Father: "And I suppose you have come to ask permission to marry her?"
Young man: "No, sir. I came to ask you to make her behave herself."

~

It looks like we are enjoying more prosperity than most of us can afford.

~

A lot of folks are down on what they are not up on.

~

It's funny where they give you a shot for a cold in the head.

~

A fellow from Texas cashed a check so big that the bank bounced.

~

A fellow read so much about the terrible effects of smoking that he decided to stop reading.

~

I read about a man whose wife had quadruplets — he went out and bought a fifth.

~

Eli Whitney invented the cotton gin but the people from the South wouldn't drink it.

~

Eli Whitney told his wife to keep her cotton-picking fingers out of his gin.

~

No formal dinner is complete without nuts — you should always invite a few.

~

Lulu went window-shopping and returned with five windows.

~

Lulu gets unlimited mileage out of a limited vocabulary.

~

Sign on a dentist's door: "Get your 1998 plates here."

~

I hope you smile at some of my jokes and wisecracks. Your grandfather did.

~

Lulu couldn't tell her twins apart, so she took them to a tattoo artist and had him put "Jane" on one and "John" on the other.

~

Gus says folks may live and learn, but by the time they've learned, it's usually too late to live.

~

He: "What's that gurgling I hear?"
She: "It's me trying to swallow that line you're throwing my way."

~

Science teacher: "Today we will discuss the heart, lungs and liver."
Student: "Gosh, just another organ recital."

~

The money gals invest in beauty aids draws the most interest.

~

Sound opinions don't make a lot of noise.

~

Gus says folks ought to live within their means even if they have to borrow the money to do so.

~

Herb: "What do you think of Red China?"
Louise: "I think red china would go good with a white tablecloth."

~

Fishing is a favorite sport of man. Women prefer angling.

~

We celebrated our survival of the old year.

~

Tired of ranch life, while in town one day a Texas cowhand saw a sign in the post office, Man Wanted for Bank Robbery. He went in to apply for the job.

~

Attorney: "Now, tell the jury just where the defendant was milking his cow."
Sweet young witness: "I think it was just a little ways back from the center of the cow."

~

Ella returned all of her boyfriend's letters stamped, "fourth class male."

~

Gus says folks always in a hurry can pass up more than they catch up with.

Gus says folks ought to live within their means even if they have to borrow the money to do so.

~

All those good things come to the other fellow if you wait long enough.

~

Many modern girls may not know how to cook, but they sure know what's cooking.

~

We would like to buy one of those small foreign cars, but our little daughter has a habit of putting things in her mouth.

~

You don't cool an engine by stripping the gears.

~

In China, they don't hang men with wooden legs — they use a rope.

~

Before inflation set in, she had a million-dollar figure.

~

Lester: "Do you have insect problems in your corn?"
Roland: "No, if I get insects in my corn, I fish them out and drink it anyway."

~

Gus says he hopes nobody tells the hens how much a bricklayer gets for laying bricks.

~

Most girls have Santa beat by a mile when it comes to filling stockings.

~

Almost every nation in the world now has a Santa Claus, but in some nations it's called "foreign aid."

~

A fellow sure has to use his noodle these days to keep out of the soup.

~

Harry: "Are you the oldest in your family?"
Roland: "No, Ma and Pa are older."

~

Some folks who put up a big front may be a little behind.

~

Sven: "We are having a raffle for a poor widow. Will you buy a ticket?"
Ole: "No, Lena wouldn't let me keep her if I won."

∼

Lulu: "Ordinarily I don't chase a man, but this one was getting away."

∼

Women don't mind the government putting only men's faces on money as long as they can get their hands on it.

∼

Husband to wife: "If someone makes fun of your bikini, don't try to laugh it off."

∼

If it weren't for venetian blinds, it would be curtains for many of us.

∼

George: "Has speed reading helped you?"
Walter: "Yes, I no longer find myself in the ladies' rest room."

∼

Lulu says when she goes to college she intends to major in annual husbandry.

∼

Hostess: "Would you care for a hot cookie?"
Alex: "No, thanks, I brought my own date."

∼

Lester: "Do you have to make that noise while you're playing tennis?"
Gus: "How can you play tennis without raising a racket?"

∼

Doctor: "I can't find anything wrong with you. I think it is due to drinking."
Roland: "Okay, Doc. I'll come back when you're sober."

∼

Alex: "How was iron discovered?"
Lester: "They smelt it."

∼

Some fishermen don't catch anything until they get home.

∼

Christmas carol: "While shepherds washed their socks at night."

∼

Sign on the house of a Justice of the Peace: "Are you fit to be tied?"

~

Clifford: "When I shave in the morning, I feel ten years younger."
Sophie: "Why don't you shave in the evening?"

~

The best way to put down crime is to stop putting up with it.

~

Teacher: "What is commonly raised in countries that have wet climates?"
Kirsten: "Umbrellas."

~

Sophie: "You look like Helen Green."
Maggie: "I look worse in pink."

~

A taxi driver stopped when he heard the young lady say stop. He continued to drive when she informed the driver that she was not talking to him.

~

A racetrack is a place where the windows clean people.

~

It's during the football season that girls whistle at men in sweaters.

~

We have two janitors at school who are broom mates. They swept together for years.

~

Customs officer: "Lady, you said this bag contained clothes, but it's full of brandy."
Lady: "Certainly, my husband's nightcaps."

~

Ella: "I'm going out tonight with a used car salesman."
Maggie: "What's the difference, new or used, as long as he's healthy."

~

Jim is one of our early settlers — he always pays his bills promptly.

~

New lady next door: "Sonny, I need a dozen eggs from the store. Do you suppose you could go for me?"
Sonny: "No, but I heard Gus say he could."

~

Guys are often popular when they have money; women can be popular when they're busted.

~

Sign in a tailor shop: "If your pants have an iron deficiency, we'll press them for you."

∽

Keep your head above water — stay away from expensive dives.

∽

Angry neighbor: "Did you tell your son to stop mimicking me?"
Mother: "Yes, I told him to stop acting like a fool."

∽

She is so lazy she won't even exercise discretion.

∽

A person who has everything should be quarantined.

∽

A man possesses only one-tenth horsepower on a sustained basis and one-half horsepower in spurts.

∽

"Freeze a jolly good fellow" is the title of an Eskimo song.

∽

Jerry: "What is the best thing out?"
Tom: "An aching tooth."

∽

Alex: "Why does the stork stand on one leg?"
Roland: "If he lifted his other leg, he'd fall down."

∽

Harry: "What instrument do you play at home?"
Roland: "Second fiddle."

∽

Roland says, "If you don't feel well, you've lost your sense of touch."

∽

Clerk to lady trying on form-fitting sweater: "Do you want to step outside and try it out for whistles?"

∽

Nurse: "Good morning. I'm the new nurse."
Patient: "Are you a trained nurse?"
Nurse: "Yes, of course I'm trained."
Patient: "Let's see you do some tricks."

∽

Medical college instructor: "This young man limps because one leg is shorter than the other. Harry, what would you do in such a case?"
Harry: "I'd limp, too."

~

Fireman: "Come to our dance and we'll come to your fire."

~

Playing golf brings taxes to mind. You drive hard to get to the green and then wind up in the hole.

~

Cute girl to potential employer: "Be-fore I accept this job, I think it is only fair to tell you that there won't be any opportunities for advances."

~

Girls are minors up to age twenty-one, but some are gold diggers all their lives.

~

Attorney: "Where did the car hit you?"
Lady: "Well, if I had been wearing a license plate, it would have been badly damaged."

~

A man that makes his money in crooked dough is a pretzel bender.

~

"You should see what I saw," said the carpenter.

~

Roland at a ladies' store: "I want a bra for my wife."
Clerk: "What bust?"
Roland: "Nothing, it just wore out."

~

Sophie: "That's a pretty dress you have on."
Lulu: "Yes, I wear it only to teas."
Sophie: "To tease whom?"

~

Loose management can get you into a tight fix.

~

Our dog is just like one of the family — I'm not saying which one.

~

Clifford: "How about some old-fashioned loving?"
Sophie: "Okay. I'll call Grandma."

~

Little girls spend their money on suckers and suckers spend their money on big girls.

~

Gus says fatal diseases kill more people than any other kind.

~

Roland: "Where did Webster get all those words he put in the dictionary?"
Lulu: "He had an argument with his wife, I think.

∽

No one seems to be sure about the stock market. It's not the bulls and the bears that bother me — it's the bum steers.

∽

Clerk: "This whiskey is seven years old."
Old lady: "If it's so damn good, why didn't someone buy it seven years ago?"

∽

Funeral home sign: "Our service is out of this world. So are our customers."

∽

She reminds me of a girl I used to sleep with — in English class.

∽

"Who are those people cheering?" asked the recruit as the soldiers marched away. "Those," said the wise old sergeant, "are the people who are not going."

∽

Uncle Jeff went to Las Vegas in a $33,000 Cadillac and came home in a $189,000 Greyhound bus.

∽

She: "I don't look forty, do I?"
He: "Not anymore."

∽

Luscious-looking librarian: "Sorry, I don't have that book."
Lady: "That's peculiar. My husband said you had everything."

∽

Trap shooting is America's favorite sport.

∽

When people lose faith in God, they turn to what looks like the next most powerful thing, the state. How bad a choice the state is, let Russians testify.

∽

In 1950, President Harry Truman predicted that by the year 2,000 the average family income would be $12,000 a year.

∽

What happened to the money we were going to save by not smoking?

~

Joe: "Were you injured in the melee?"
Jack: "No, I was kicked in the ribs."

~

Whether or not boys make passes at girls with glasses depends on their frames.

~

A prominent doctor pointed out that babies are born to one out of every four people in hospitals. Therefore, if you have been in the hospital three times, you'd better look out.

~

I eat my peas with honey. I've done it all my life. It makes the peas taste funny, but they stick well to my knife.

~

Notice: This year's Christmas party will be canceled on account of last year's Christmas party.

~

Fast driving can bring places closer together — like this world and the next.

~

He is as changeable as a baby's underwear.

~

There is nothing wrong with him that a straightjacket wouldn't cure.

~

She was only a candy counter girl, but she knew her suckers.

~

Lester: "I want a girl who doesn't smoke, drink, swear or play around."
Ernest: "What for?"

~

The hotel reservation clerk opened the telegram and read, "Do you have any accommodations where I can put up with my wife?"

~

Oscar is an ill-humored civil engineer who always builds crossroads.

~

Our postmaster bought himself a brand new Lincoln. How can he do that when his business has been running at a loss for years?

~

Joe: "That college turns out some great men."
Bill: "When did you graduate?"
Joe: "I didn't graduate. I was turned out."

∼

Lady: "I want to buy some traveler's checks."
Teller: "What denomination?"
Lady: "Baptist."

∼

Flo: "My cabin on the ship was nice, but I didn't like the washing machine."
Joe: "Washing machine? That's a porthole."
Flo: "No wonder I never got my clothes back."

∼

Pretty girl: "Can you squeeze me in there?"
Bus driver: "It will be a pleasure if I can get someone to drive this bus."

∼

That girl is a real live wire. She gives everyone in the office a shock.

∼

Father: "When I was a young man, girls knew how to blush."
Daughter: "What did you say to them, Dad?"

∼

If it were as easy to arouse enthusiasm as it is to arouse suspicion, just think what could be accomplished.

∼

A mother hen saw a platter of scrambled eggs and remarked, "You crazy mixed-up kids."

∼

My money talks — it says good-bye.

∼

Half of our life is spent trying to find something to do with the time we saved rushing through it.

∼

My son takes after his mother. I used to do the same thing.

∼

I'm telling this story ... because I remember it.

∼

Lena took Ole to the doctor for an examination. She didn't think he was up to par. The doctor examined Ole and exclaimed, "I want a urine, a stool and a sperm specimen."
Ole: "Lena, what does he mean?"
Lena: "He wants your dirty undershorts."

~

When a guy sits on a tack, he's better off.

~

Not all the folks in America came over on the same ship, but they're all in the same boat now.

~

The young lad took the bus home from school, but his mother made him take it back.

~

Harry says a humorist is a smart fellow who originates old jokes.

~

Why are those girls making eyes at the quarterback? He's not making those passes at them.

~

In spring, a young man's fancy turns to income tax and other forms.

~

Lawyer: "Well, do you want my honest opinion?"
Client: "No, no, I want your professional advice."

~

Last month I received five parking tickets. I went to the city clerk and asked for a season ticket.

~

Nice lady to little girl: "You're pretty dirty, aren't you?"
Kirsten: "Yes, but I'm prettier when I'm clean."

~

Women have been known for untold ages.

~

Janitor: "I'll bet you see some strange sights."
Window washer: "Yes, there's an office on the sixth floor where everyone is always working."

~

Most busy folks don't have time to be busybodies.

~

Little girl: "Someday somebody will start a war and nobody will come."

~

According to sales reports, our automobile companies had a bang-up year. According to accident reports, so did their customers.

∾

Lawyer: "Do you believe in capital punishment?"
Young juror: "Well, yes, if it isn't too severe."

∾

It doesn't seem fair when you pay thirty-five dollars to take your girl-friend to a football game and watch some other guy make all the passes.

∾

Alex: "We always meet together in groups of five."
Gus: "Alex means whenever those four meet, they have a fifth."

∾

I just now realized that both repub-licans and sinners are mentioned in the Bible, but not a word about democrats. St. Paul is also men-tioned in the Bible, but again, not a word about Minneapolis.

∾

She: "I guess I'm just a babe in the woods."
He: "Honey, meet an old forest ranger."

∾

I pity the poor hen. She never finds things where she lays them.

∾

Ernie: "Why does the state of Missouri stand at the head of mule raising?"
Roland: "Because the other end is too dangerous."

∾

Teacher: "If you subtract 14 from 116, what's the difference?"
Tommy: "Yes, I think it's a lot of foolishness too."

∾

Alex: "How old is your grand-mother?"
Roland: "I don't know, but we've had her for a long, long time."

∾

This party is dull, let's leave.
I can't. I'm the host.

∾

A babysitter is a teenager who comes in to act like an adult while the adults go out and act like teenagers.

∾

Some people think it's impolite to walk out of a party, but it may be better to walk out than to be carried out.

∾

~

Sally: "That's a pretty coat you have."
Janis: "Thanks, my husband gave it to me on my thirtieth birthday."
Sally: "Wears well, doesn't it?"

~

Ladies' bridge foursome is usually good for a slam or two of one kind or another.

~

Willard gave up smoking and started chewing toothpicks. Now he has Dutch elm disease.

~

What becomes of furniture that's too old for poor folks and not yet old enough for rich folks?

~

Nothing but money and kisses that are loaded with germs could remain so popular.

~

Morticians have a layaway plan.

~

Bikinis are used more for hunting than swimming.

~

Some folks look ahead, some look back, some just look confused.

~

Language is the apparel in which our thoughts parade before the public. Let's never clothe them in vulgar or shoddy attire.

~

People with a one-track mind often have a derailed train of thought.

~

Saving money these days is as hard as playing a trumpet from the wrong end.

~

Judge: "You've been brought here for drinking."
Patrick: "Okay, judge, let's get started."

~

Give credit to the egotists. They don't talk about other people.

~

First golfer: "What's your handicap?"
Second golfer: "Honesty."

~

Sam: "I'm from the south. I think faster than I talk."
Jeff: "I wish I could do that."

~

An easy way to obtain a small business is to buy a large business, then be patient while you wait.

~

The dalmatian's job fighting a fire is to point out the fireplug.

~

I'll never forget what's-his-name.

~

I read that in California a man is run over every half hour. Poor fellow.

~

A man was out in his yard with a telescope looking at the stars. A drunk came by and asked him what he was doing. "I'm looking at the stars," was his answer. At that moment, the drunk looked up. Both witnessed a falling star. The drunk remarked, "Good shot."

~

The church had a congregational meeting to decide on some chandeliers for the church. The meeting dragged on for two hours without anything constructive development. Finally one fellow in the back of the church said, "I'm against all of this. First of all, no one knows how to spell chandelier; and another thing, nobody knows how to play it. If we spend money for anything, we should buy some lights."

~

A construction company that had great pride in their efficiency called a special conference in order to find out why one brick was left over from the day before on a commercial building. The foreman was asked, "Where does this brick belong?" The foreman took the brick and threw it out the window. "Go on to the next story."

~

A wealthy lady flying first class managed to get her little dog on board the plane without being reported by the stewardess. During the flight, the little old lady complained about the captain's cigar smoke. When the captain was confronted with the smelly cigar, the captain and the old lady negotiated, resulting in a deal as follows: "I'll throw out this cigar if you'll throw out your dog." The problem was settled. After landing, the passengers looked out the window. There was the dog sitting on a wing of the airplane. Guess what the dog had in his mouth ... the brick from the preceding story.

∽

A farmer's barn had just burned to the ground. The insurance agent explained to the farmer, "According to your insurance policy, our company will build you another barn exactly like the barn that was destroyed, but you will not be able to collect cash." The farmer exclaimed, "If that's the way you people do business, you can cancel the policy on my wife."

∽

A bar of steel with a value of eight dollars made into horseshoes is worth twenty-four dollars; made into needles, it's worth five thousand dollars, and if turned into fine watch springs, it's worth three hundred thousand dollars. The value of people can be increased immeasurably by what is made of them.

∽

A young fellow was asked, "What happened to you?" He explained, "I was at a real estate seminar. The speaker stopped speaking to give everyone a stretch break. I noticed that the lady in front of me had her dress caught in her seat. Being a serious minded guy, I pulled it out. She swung around and hit me with her purse. That caught my left eye."
"How do you account for your right eye also being black?"
"Well, since she felt so positive about the dress location, when we had the next stretch break, I put the dress back in."

∽

A young married couple bought a parakeet, but all he could say was, "Let's neck." The preacher heard about it and suggested that they put his bird, who always said "Let's pray" in the cage with the delinquent bird, and maybe it could teach the other to say "Let's pray." When the two birds were put together, the couple's bird said, "Let's neck." The preacher's bird said, "My prayers have been answered."

~

A salesman fell in love with a cigarette girl but thought he should have a character report before popping the question. The detective's report: "Fine reputation, past without a blemish, has a circle of impeccable friends. Only breath of scandal is that lately she's been going around with a salesman of doubtful reputation."

~

A United States soldier was playing cards with some English soldiers for the first time. Taking a quick look at what he had been dealt, the GI saw four aces. "One pound" was the bet ventured by the Englishman on his right. "I don't know how you count your money," said the G.I., "but I'll raise you a ton."

~

A young student from agricultural college was visiting an old farmer. He stated: "Your farming methods are so old and behind the times that I would be surprised if you got a hundred dollars out of this field of oats."
Farmer: "I also would be surprised. I seeded barley."

~

Paying no attention to the red traffic light, the whizzing cars, or the policeman's outraged whistle, the little old lady marched across the street. Horns blasted, brakes squealed, and the cop angrily strode up to her. "Say, lady," he growled, "didn't you see my hand raised? Don't you know what that means?"
"Well, of course I do," she snapped. "I've been teaching school for twenty-five years."

~

When a country doctor climbed into the seat of his very old car, some youths were standing around laughing at the old car. The doctor said mildly, "At least this car is paid for." He looked deliberately from one boy to another. "You're not, and neither are you."

~

A farmer flying for the first time in his life gladly accepted chewing gum from the flight attendant. "This will keep your ears from popping when we attain a high altitude," she said. After the plane landed, the farmer approached her. "Thank you for the gum. I have one question though. How do I get it out of my ears?"

～

The attorney was questioning a farmer regarding a bodily injury claim. "Why did you tell the sheriff that you never felt better in your life?"

"You see," he replied, "when the sheriff arrived, he saw my horse with a broken leg and he shot it. Since my dog Rover was all banged up, he shot him dead, too. So, when he asked me how I was feeling, I said I'd never felt better in my life. Under such circumstances, I thought that was a wise choice of words."

～

A meek little man in a restaurant timidly touched the arm of a large man picking up an overcoat. "Excuse me, but do you happen to be Mr. Smith of Rochester?"

"No, I'm not!" the large man answered impatiently.

"Oh, er, well," stammered the little man, "I am, and that's his coat you picked up.

～

One of the unmarried girls who works in a busy office arrived early one morning and began passing out cigars and candy, all tied with blue ribbons. When asked what the occasion was, she proudly displayed a diamond on her third finger, left hand, and announced, "It's a boy — six feet tall and a hundred and eighty-seven pounds."

～

Mother took off little Jimmy's pants and went to work on them with needle and thread. Suddenly she realized that Jimmy was gone and started to look for him. Hearing a noise in the basement, she went to the stairway and called, "Are you running around down there without any pants?"

"No, ma'am," came the reply. "I'm reading the gas meter."

~

A husband helping his wife clean chickens soon learned that after pulling the main feathers out, many small hair-like feathers remained. He thought there must be a better way to give it the final touch and soon went to get his Schick razor. That razor really did the job. With this type of result, he thought the Schick people should be willing to offer an award for finding another use for their product. He carefully drafted a letter, then mailed it to the razor company. Ten days later, their decision arrived in the mail as follows: "Dear Erv, we have a ladies' Schick and a men's Schick, but we are not interested in any chicken Schick."

~

A businessman told his secretary that he didn't want any visitors or any interruptions. "If anybody says that their business is important, just say, 'That's what they all say.' That afternoon a woman came in and insisted on seeing the boss. "I am his wife," she said. "That's what they all say," replied the secretary.

~

A lady from Dallas went for a swim. After a few minutes, she lost the top of her swimsuit. She was very embarrassed and crossed her arms in front of her as she came out of the water. Little Sven was watching and remarked, "Lady, if you're going to drown those puppies, I'll take the one with the pink nose."

~

Clifford was carrying a rock, a chicken and a pail, and asked Sophie to open the gate. She declined saying, "You might make a pass at me." Clifford snorted, "How could I make a pass at you with a rock, a chicken and a pail in my arms?" Sophie replied, "Well, you could set the pail over the chicken and place the rock on top of the pail."

~

Ole and Lena lived on a farm. Ole had a new outhouse built because the old one was so worn out. Rather than take the time to tear down the old one, he had the hired man put a stick of dynamite inside the building. As they prepared to detonate the charge from a hundred yards away by remote control, Lena came out of the house heading towards the outhouse. (The men forgot to tell Lena what their plans were.) Consequently, when Lena sat down, almost immediately the dynamite charge went off, blowing Lena and everything else sky-high. As Lena brushed herself off, she said, "It sure was a good ting I didn't do dat inside da house."

~

Dear Ole:

I'm not sure you will be interested in dis, but it could make you a lot of money vit a small investment of $50,000. Since you own dat fleet of herring boats, I taut you got enough money to swing it.

I am inviting yust a few good friends to invest vit me in a large cat ranch near Oslo, Norway. We vould start vit about a million cats. Each cat averages about twenty cents for the white ones and up to forty cents for the black ones. Dis vill give us 12 million cat skins per year to sell for an average of thirty-two cents, making our gross revenue about four million dollars a year. Dis averages out to be about $11,000 a day, including Sundays and holidays.

A good Norwegian cat man can skin about fifty cats, working part time each day for $3.15. It vill take 663 men to operate the ranch, so dat net profit vould be over $9,200 per day. Our $50,000 investment vould be recovered in 5.3 days.

Da cats vould be fet on rats exclusively. Rats multiply four times as fast as cats. Ve vould start a rat ranch adjacent to our cat farm. If ve start vit a million rats, ve vill have four rats per cat per day. Da rats vill be fet on da carcasses of da cats dat ve skin. Dis vill give each rat a quarter of a cat. You can see da business is clean, self-supporting and automatic. Da cats vill eat da rats and da rats vill eat da cats and ve vill get da skins.

Eventually, I hope to cross da cats vit snakes so dey vill skin demselves twice a year. Dis vould save da labor cost of skinning as vell as give us two skins for each cat. Let me know if your are interested, Ole. I am radder choosy about who gets into dis skinning operation. I am reserving a very attractive engraved certificate dat I vill send you upon receipt of your cash for vhatever share of da operation you vant to own. Cash only. No checks.

Your buddy, Knute.

~

A Norwegian girl competed with a French and an English girl in the breaststroke swim competition. The French girl came in first; the English girl second. The Norwegian girl came in last and was completely exhausted. After being revived, she remarked, "I don't want to complain, but I think those other two girls used their arms."

~

A fellow wanted to see the Olympics. Instead of going to the spectators' gate, he arrived at the contestants' gate. The guard said, "Are you a pole vaulter?" He replied, "No, I'm a Norwegian. How did you know my name was Valter?"

~

Roland went to the doctor for a physical complaining about his sex performance. The doctor told him to walk ten miles a day and call him in a week. A week later, Roland called the doctor. "How is your sex life?" asked the doctor. "What sex? I'm seventy miles from home."

~

Ole called the doctor and asked him to remove buckshot from his son-in-law's rear quarters. The doctor asked, "Why in the world would you fire buckshot at your son-in-law?" To which Ole replied, "When I fired the buckshot, he wasn't my son-in-law."

~

Ole came home one night inebriated. Acting feisty, Ole said to Lena, "Lena, you remind me of a John Deere tractor." Lena chose to ignore him and went about fixing Ole's supper. Later, Ole said, "Lena, on second thought, you remind me of a Massey-Ferguson combine." Again Lena ignored him, since Ole was usually argumentative after drinking. But the supper mellowed Ole out somewhat and by bedtime, he was in a very good mood. In fact, after turning out the lights, Ole said, "Lena, how about you and me having some fun?" Lena said, "Ole, if you think I'm going to start up this eighty-five thousand dollar combine for just a half an ear of corn, you're crazy."

~

A young lady, just back from a horseback ride, was in a local department store to buy some talcum powder. She asked the floorwalker to direct her. The floorwalker said, "Just walk this way, madam." The young lady, observing his walk, remarked, "If I could walk that way, I wouldn't need the talcum powder."

∼

The toastmaster introduced the speaker, wiped his wet brow with his napkin and lowered his 220 odd pounds gratefully into his chair. The speaker said, "Gentlemen, in our country we have a lovely fable. When a baby is born, its guardian angel bestows a kiss. If the kiss is on the brow, the child will be greatly intellectual. If it is on the eyes, it will be a great beauty. If it is on the fingers, it will be a great artist. I can't tell you where our presiding officer was kissed by his guardian angel, but he really makes a great chairman."

∼

Two young ladies were discussing their dads. One bragged, "My dad is handsome, smart and influential." The other replied, "My dad is not only handsome, smart and influential, but he is a great artist. He has produced one of the greatest wonders in the modern world." The first asked, "What did he ever produce that is so great?" The other tossed her head, spun around and said, "Look me over, kid, look me over."

∼

The tobacco industry reports that it provides jobs for two-and-a-half million Americans. This figures does not include doctors, x-ray technicians, nurses, hospital workers, firefighters, pharmacists, morticians and grave diggers.

∼

A bachelor was bragging that he'd been out on a date every evening — Monday with Edith, Tuesday with Caroline, Wednesday with Fido. His friends stopped him right there and said, "Fido sounds like a dog." The bachelor moaned, "If you think Fido's a dog, you should see Edith and Caroline."

∼

A gentleman was looking for a parrot that could speak two languages. He searched for several months. One day the operator of the local pet shop called him and said that he had such a parrot. On arriving at the pet shop, the operator informed the prospective customer that the parrot spoke not just two languages, but five. He was delighted. He purchased the parrot and told the owner to send the cage and parrot to his home and his wife would be there to receive the parrot. When the purchaser arrived home that evening, he asked his wife, "What are we having for dinner?"

"You should ask," she replied. "You sent it home this afternoon."

"Do you mean to tell me, dear, that you cooked the parrot I sent home? The one I've been searching for for such a long time? Did you know that the parrot could speak not only two languages, but five?"

"Why didn't he speak up, then?" asked the wife.

≈

Ole the brush salesman stopped at a house to sell brushes. The lady of the house said she did not need brushes. Ole said, "Lady, these are not just ordinary brushes, and to prove that point, I'll leave a floor brush, a toilet brush and a hairbrush. When I return next week, you can buy one, two, or all three, or you may return all three." The following week Ole returned. "Would you like to keep some of these brushes," he asked. The lady replied, "Yes, I would like to keep the hairbrush and the floor brush, but not the toilet brush." Ole asked, "Don't you like the toilet brush?" The lady responded, "No, I prefer to use toilet paper."

≈

Dear Son:

Yust a few lines to let you know that I am still alive. I am writing this letter slowly becoss I know you can't read fast. You won't know the house when you come home. Ve have moved. Ve had trouble moving — especially the bed. The man wouldn't let us take it in the taxi. It maybe wouldn't have been so bad if your father hadn't been in it at the time. Speaking of your father, he has a new yob. He has five hundred men under him. He cuts grass at the cemetery. Your sister got engaged last veek. Her boyfriend gave her a beautiful ring with three stones missing. Our neighbors are now raising pigs. Ve yust got vind of it this morning.

I suppose you didn't know I got my appendix out and a dishwasher put in.

Ve found a vash machine in our new house, but it doesn't vork so good. Last veek, I put in four shirts, pulled the chain and ve haven't seen the shirts since. Your sister Ingrid had a baby yesterday. I haven't heard if is a boy or a girl, so I can't say yet if you are an aunt or an uncle. Uncle Throvale vent to Minneapolis to vork in a bloomer factory. Ve hear he is pulling down seventy-five a veek. Your Aunt Tina got a yob in St. Paul vorking in a factory. I'm sending her some clean underwear as she says she has been in the same shift since she got there.

Your father didn't have too much to drink at Christmas. I put some castor oil in his whisky and it kept him going until New Years. I vent to the doctor on Thursday. Your pa came with me. The doctor put a glass tube in my mouth and said to keep it shut for ten minutes. Later on, your pa asked to buy it from him. On Monday, it was so vindy one of our chickens laid the same egg four times. I must close now. There's a big sale downtown and vomen's bloomers are half off.

Your loving mother

P.S. I vas going to send you ten dollars but I already sealed the envelope.

≈

A drunk came up the aisle on an Amtrack coach and said, "Hey, lady, you have the homeliest ba ba baby I have ever seen." The lady was very insulted and hurt. She told the conductor of her intent to sue the railroad company. The conductor said, "Now, lady, just relax. We'll confine the drunk now and remove him from the train at the next station. In the meantime, I'll buy you the best steak on the train and I'll even provide some bananas for your monkey."

≈

Christopher Columbus was the world's most remarkable salesman. He started out not knowing where he was going. When he got there, he didn't know where he was. When he returned, he didn't know where he had been. He did all this on borrowed money and managed to get a repeat order.

≈

A new and better mousetrap: An inventor used a lead pipe as a passageway and cut across the pipe at an angle, inserted a razor blade and, beyond that, a piece of cheese was placed. The mouse would enter just beyond the razor blade to eat the cheese. After eating the cheese, the mouse, while backing up, would cut off his head. The patent office disapproved this trap as follows: (1) the lead pipe presents an ecology problem; (2) OSHA considers the razor blade an accident hazard. The inventor was sure that the mousetrap was sound in theory. This time around, instead of the lead pipe and razor blade, he used a copper pipe and a hacksaw section and did not use cheese. The mouse gets into position as stated above. Now while looking from left to right saying, "Where is the cheese?" he hacks off his head.

~

Ole decided to become a railroad engineer. He took a special course on how to handle a locomotive. Ole passed his written test. He then had to pass an oral test. The examiner asked, "Assuming you are in full charge propelling the train down the track at sixty miles per hour and you receive a radio message telling you that there is another train on the same track going in the opposite direction. What would you do?"
Ole: "I'd call Sven."
Examiner: "Why would you call Sven under these circumstances?"
Ole: "Sven has never seen a train wreck."

~

Lena went to the doctor for a checkup. The doctor said there seemed to be a slight heart problem and advised her to take some pills for two weeks and then come back. "Most of all, don't climb any stairs," advised the doctor. "We have a two-story house," said Lena. "Well, I understand that," said the doctor, "but it's important that you not climb any stairs." Two weeks later, Lena came back and the doctor pronounced her hale and hearty. "Can I climb stairs again?" asked Lena. "Of course," said the doctor. "Good," said Lena, "because I was getting tired of climbing up that drainpipe every night."

~

A hearse going down a steep hill went out of control and turned over. The coffin and occupant flew out, bounced down the hill, slid across the street and flew through the window of a drugstore. It continued to the rear where it upended against the prescription counter. The top flew off and the occupant sat up. "May I help you?" the druggist politely asked. "Yes," said the occupant. "Give me something to stop this coffin."

∼

A hillbilly came to town carrying a jug of spirits in one hand and a shotgun in the other. He stopped a man on the street, saying, "Here, friend, take a drink out of my jug." The man protested that he did not drink. The hillbilly leveled his shotgun at the stranger and said, "Drink." The stranger drank, then shuddered, shook, shivered and coughed. "Gad, that's awful stuff!" "Ain't it?" said the hillbilly. "Now, hold the gun on me while I take a gulp."

∼

A fellow walked into a doctor's office and the receptionist asked him what he had. He said "shingles." She took down his name, address, medical insurance number, and asked him to have a seat. Fifteen minutes later, a nurse's aide came out and asked him what he had. He said "shingles," so she took down his weight, a complete medical history, and told him to wait in an examining room. A short time later, a nurse came in and asked him what he had. He said "shingles." She gave him a blood test, a blood pressure test, and told him to take off all his clothes and wait for the doctor. An hour later, the doctor came in and asked what he had, and he said "shingles." The doctor asked "where." He said, "Outside in the truck. Where do you want them?"

∼

Ole and Lena won a contest. The prize was a trip around the world. When they arrived in Russia, they were assigned a special guide named Rudolph. As Rudolph was showing them around Red Square, it started to rain a bit. Then some sleet came down. "Yee viss," exclaimed Ole, "here comes da snow." "Oh, no," said Rudolph the Russian, "it is rain." "And I say it is snow," retorted Ole. Lena, trying to be the diplomat, said, "Now, now, Ole, calm down. After all, Rudolph the Red knows rain, dear."

∼

An Englishman put it this way: "We should behave toward our country as loving women behave toward their men. A loving wife will do anything for her husband except stop criticizing him and trying to improve him. We should cast the same affectionate but sharp glance at our country. We should love it but insist upon telling it all its faults. The noisy, empty patriot, not the critic, is the dangerous citizen."

≈

You can't always win. A man met a friend he hadn't seen for two years and asked him about his wife. "She went to heaven two years ago," said his friend. "Oh, I'm so sorry," said the man. Thinking he should not have said he was sorry that the man's wife went to heaven, he said, "No, I'm glad." That sounded even worse, so he blurted out, "No, I'm surprised."

≈

A five-year-old asked Grandma, "How old are you?"
"Now, Robert," Grandma said, "you must not ask a lady her age."
A while later, Robert asked, "Grandma, how much do you weigh?"
"Robert, you must not ask the weight, either."
The next day, Robert noticed his Grandma's billfold on the end table open with her driver's license exposed. "Grandma, you are fifty-four years old, you weigh 155 pounds, and you got an F in sex."

≈

Two golfers found a golfer in a daze on the fairway with a number seven iron wrapped around his neck. They brought him to the clubhouse, gave him a cold drink, and made the proper introductions. After he could talk, they asked, "What happened out there?"
John: "I was out alone today to practice up a bit. There were these two ladies hitting their balls all over the place, wasting time and visiting. They didn't offer to let me play through and I did everything to be a perfect gentleman. Finally, they hit a ball into the cow pasture. I went to help them find the ball so we all could proceed with the golf game. I noticed a ball stuck in the back end of the cow. All I did was lift up the cow's tail and ask, does this look like yours? She swung that darn number seven iron at me."

≈

A man walked up to the desk of a resort hotel and asked for a room. "Do you have a reservation?" asked the indifferent clerk.

Guest: "No, but I've been coming here every year for twelve years and I've never had to have a reservation."

Clerk: "Well, there is nothing available. We are filled up and without a reservation, you can't get a room."

Guest: "Suppose the president of the United States came in. You would have a room for him, wouldn't you?"

Clerk: "Of course, for the President we would have room."

Guest: "All right. Now I'm telling you that the president isn't coming here tonight, so give me his room."

AGING

More people worry about the future than prepare for the future.

∼

The last thing we seem to learn in life is to put first things first.

∼

Either I'm becoming overweight or I'm too short.

∼

Wrinkles are hereditary. Parents get them from their children.

∼

Don't let the future scare you — it's just as shaky as you are.

∼

About the only thing that comes to him who waits is old age.

∼

If you really believe old soldiers fade away, try getting into your old army uniform.

∼

The reason time goes faster when you are older is because you are going downhill.

∼

If you feel your corn more than your oats, you're getting old.

∼

There are many old codgers around who still drive a car, and maybe a lot more who aren't around because they did.

∼

I remember a few things that I would rather forget.

∼

I feel just as good at seventy-seven as I did at seventy-six.

∼

Golf is a sport where a small white ball is chased by men too old to chase anything else.

∼

I shave, get haircuts and comb my hair to improve on Mother Nature, but I can't fool Father Time.

∼

Sophie had an hourglass figure until the sands of time shifted.

∼

When you're over the hill, enjoy the view.

≈

How does a fellow get over the hill without ever being on top?

≈

The best way to look young is to hang around with older people.

≈

By the time a man finds greener pastures, he is too old to climb the fence.

≈

You know you're getting old when instead of avoiding temptation, temptation avoids you.

≈

A pretty young girl was going to have some fun with a ninety-four-year-old man. She said, "Would you like some super sex?" The old man replied, "I'll take the soup."

≈

For every man over ninety, there are ten women, but it's too late then.

≈

When you are older, you must cut down on many activities. It's the same with sex. I now only talk about sex half as much.

≈

By the time you have money to burn, you're too old to play with matches.

≈

By the time opportunity knocks, you'll probably have your hearing aid turned off.

≈

You're getting old when it takes longer to rest up than to get tired.

≈

Middle age is when your memory is shorter, your experience longer, stamina lower and your forehead is higher.

≈

Old golfers never die — they just lose their drive.

≈

The good old days were better because we were younger then.

≈

You're sure to grow older, but you don't have to get old.

≈

Old age: bifocals, bunions, bridges, bulges and baldness.

~

Wrinkles indicate where smiles have been.

~

There are few things as rare as a well spent life.

~

We don't stop laughing because we grow old. We grow old because we stop laughing.

~

If I can live beyond the age of a hundred and three, I'll have it made. Few people die after that age.

~

I have better things to do than to merely grow old.

~

When all you exercise is caution, you're getting old.

~

The process of growing old is a question of mind over matter. If you don't mind, it doesn't matter.

~

You are old if you can remember when the village square was a place, not a person.

~

The years Lulu subtracts from her age are not lost. She adds them to the age of other women.

~

Clifford: "I'm approaching the age of thirty."
Gus: "From which direction?"

~

Junior and his mother were looking through the family album. They came to a picture of a handsome young man with a large crop of wavy hair. Junior exclaimed, "Who is that?"
"Why, that's your father," exclaimed the mother.
Skeptically, Junior asked, "Then who's the bald-headed guy that's been living with us?"

~

Sign in a restaurant: Don't make fun of our coffee. You may be old and weak yourself some day.

~

To make success of old age, a fellow must start young. If you wait too long, you'll be too old to navigate when your ship comes in.

∼

Old age is when you buy a birthday cake and the baker throws in a smoke alarm for free.

∼

A lady at age one hundred and two was asked what she enjoyed most at her age. "The lack of peer pressure," she replied.

∼

Seventy-year-old Bob: "Did you like Paris?"
Seventy-five-year-old Al: "Wonderful. I just wish I could have made the trip forty years ago."
Bob: "When Paris was really Paris?"
Al: "No, when Al was really Al."

∼

Old fellow: "Please forgive me. I'm sorry but I can't remember your name."
Second old fellow: bewildered: "How soon do you need to know?"

∼

Age is a relative matter. You are young as long as you have a relative older than you.

∼

The golf pro looked at the old man and said, "It looks to me like you might be too old to carry a bag of clubs, but you could walk along and help locate the ball. Are your eyes good?"
"Perfect," said the elderly man. "Still 20/20."
The pro proceeded to hit the ball 270 yards. "Did you see where it went?" asked the pro.
"I sure did."
Pro: "Where?"
Old man: "I forgot."

∼

An old-timer is a fellow who remembers when the only problem with parking a car was getting the girl to agree to it.

∼

Prepare for retirement. If you think you could be happy letting the government take care of you, just remember what happened to the American Indians.

∼

There are three things that are bad about getting old. Number one, you can't remember things ... and I forgot the other two.

∼

It's not all bad to be bald-headed. Now all I have to do is straighten my tie.

~

If I could sell my experiences for what they cost me, I wouldn't need social security.

~

I'm at the age that when people talk about a bag, I think of my lunch.

~

Remember, it is better to be over the hill than under it.

~

They are having an age problem. He won't act his age and she won't tell her age.

~

Regardless of how well a woman carries her years, she is bound to drop a few.

~

Don't resent growing old — many are denied the privilege.

~

Why does wisdom arrive with old age — too late to do us much good?

~

The trouble with old age is now that I know my way around, I don't feel like going.

~

When you would rather see the kitchen in good shape than a good shape in the kitchen, you're getting old.

~

The trouble with growing old is that there's not much future in it.

~

Life is an eternal struggle to keep money coming in — and teeth, hair and vital organs from coming out.

~

Sophie says she is too young for Medicare and too old for men to care.

~

Gus says, "My memory is so poor I can't even remember all the words in the Happy Birthday song."

~

Gray hair usually comes along about twenty years after you thought it would make you look distinguished.

~

Regular exercise becomes more and more important as you age. You have to be in good shape to get over the hill.

~

Old age is when you fully realize what the statute of limitations is all about.

~

Ron: "It's terrible to grow old alone. My wife hasn't had a birthday in ten years."

~

Having grandchildren didn't make me feel old, but the thought of being married to a grandmother did.

~

I may be old, but I can still show you some new wrinkles.

~

Many of the things I couldn't have when I was young, I no longer want.

~

The best time to tell a woman's age is when she isn't around.

~

My classmates have all gotten so fat and bald they didn't recognize me.

~

I'm at the metallic age — gold in my teeth, silver in my hair and lead in my pants.

~

As you age, you forget names, then you forget faces. Sometimes you forget to pull up your zipper and sometimes you forget to pull your zipper down.

~

A woman is as old as she looks; a man is old when he quits looking.

~

Sleeping at the wheel is a good way to keep from growing old.

~

Birthdays are nice to have, but too many of them will kill you.

~

There is one nice thing about baldness — it's neat.

~

People are like wine — age sours the bad and improves the good.

∼

All that guy ever did was grow old (106 years) and he took longer to do that than most people.

∼

I'll never have a lot of white hair. I don't have much black hair either.

∼

Youth is when you are always looking for greener fields. Middle age is when you can hardly mow the one you have.

∼

The older I get, the better I was.

∼

They call it middle age because that's where it shows up first.

∼

By the time a guy is old enough to watch his step, he's not going anywhere.

∼

Senior citizens are the nation's leading carriers of aids: hearing aids, Band-Aids, medical aids, government aids.

∼

Ole says you're getting old when:

- ▲ Your little black book contains only names ending with M.D.
- ▲ Your back goes out more often than you do.
- ▲ You decide to procrastinate, and never get around to it.
- ▲ You can recall when the only babies a politician kissed were those in their mothers' arms.
- ▲ Everything hurts and what doesn't hurt, doesn't work.
- ▲ The gleam in your eyes is from the sun hitting your bifocals.
- ▲ You feel like the night after and you haven't been anywhere.
- ▲ You get tired playing chess.
- ▲ Your children begin to look middle-aged.
- ▲ You're still chasing women but can't remember why.
- ▲ A dripping faucet causes an uncontrollable bladder urge.
- ▲ You know all the answers but nobody asks you the questions.

▲ You look forward to a dull evening.

▲ You turn out the light for economic rather than romantic reasons.

▲ You walk with your head high trying to get used to your trifocals.

▲ You sit in a rocking chair and can't get it going.

▲ Your knees buckle and your belt doesn't.

▲ You regret all those mistakes resisting temptation.

▲ After painting the town red, you have to take a long rest before putting on the second coat.

▲ Dialing long distance wears you out.

▲ You're startled the first time you are addressed as an old-timer.

▲ You remember today that your wedding anniversary was yesterday.

▲ You burn the midnight oil until 9:00 p.m.

▲ Your pacemaker makes the garage door go up when you watch a pretty girl go by.

▲ The little gray-haired lady you help across the street is your wife.

▲ You get your exercise acting as a pallbearer for your friends who exercised.

▲ You have too much room in the house and not enough room in the medicine chest.

∼

Two older ladies in a nursing home were looking for relief from the monotony of their daily routine. They decided to streak. One evening both came streaking through all the public areas of the nursing home. Two old codgers, who couldn't hear or see too well, looked up from their wheelchairs. "What was that?" asked one. "Just a couple of gals running," answered the other. "What were they wearing?" asked the first one. "Dunno," came the answer, "but whatever it was, it sure needed ironing."

BITS OF WISDOM

Evil will triumph when good men do nothing.

~

Joy is not in things; joy is in us.

~

Learn to enjoy what you have and forget about things beyond your reach.

~

Worry is interest paid on trouble before it is due.

~

You get dollars the same way you get fishing worms.

~

A rabbit's foot is a poor substitute for horse sense.

~

Measure your wealth not by the things you have but by the things you have for which you would not take money.

~

The attendance at your funeral will depend on the weather on that specific day.

~

If we have earned the right to boast, we don't have to.

~

If you are worth your salt, you don't have to tell people.

~

You get salty butter if you cry in the churn.

~

The price is what you pay; value is what you receive.

~

You don't have to know all the answers because no one is smart enough to ask you all the questions.

~

The larger a man's head gets, the easier it is to fill his shoes.

~

While praising the optimist who invented the airplane, let us not forget the pessimist who invented the parachute.

~

A smile increases your face value.

~

All sunshine makes a desert.

~

If you didn't start the day with a smile, it's still not too late to start practicing for tomorrow.

~

Nothing will wilt faster than laurels that have been rested on.

~

Learn to enjoy the little things — there are so many. If you can't enjoy what you have, how could you be happier with more?

~

Always keep your chin up, unless you are a prizefighter.

~

Ballets keep you on your toes.

~

If you can keep your head while those around you are losing theirs, you're probably the guy operating the guillotine.

~

Smell the roses before someone spreads the fertilizer.

~

A bird in the hand may be worth two in the bush, but a bird in the hand is poor table manners. A live bird in the hand calls for wearing gloves.

~

The surest way to make ends meet is to get off of your own.

~

Eat, drink and be merry and you'll become a silly, overweight alcoholic.

~

The best place to find a helping hand is at the end of your arm.

~

Things that can worry you:

Things that never happen	40%
Things we can't change	30%
Needless health worries	12%
Miscellaneous worries	10%
Real problems	8%

~

Even a bargain costs money.

~

Most of the world's supply of trouble is produced by those who produce nothing else.

~

If you take from Peter to pay Paul, you are making Peter a Paul bearer.

~

Smoking is ten times as harmful as when they first announced smoking could kill you.

~

People who keep up with the times are not clock watchers.

~

Laughter makes more people forget their troubles than a case of whiskey.

~

There is a narrow margin between keeping your chin up and sticking your neck out.

~

Names are important. A phone book without names would merely be a bunch of numbers.

~

A person is never defeated until he admits it.

~

The search for wisdom is continually conducted, especially by the wise.

~

It isn't always the ice that makes people slip. It's often what you mix with the ice.

~

People like goldfish because they like to see something with its mouth open that's not complaining.

~

Have a great aim in life and know when to pull the trigger.

~

The only people who actually like change are little babies.

~

There is a special place on this earth for people who have no problems. It's called a cemetery.

~

It's what we learn after we know it all that counts.

~

An unusual amount of common sense is called wisdom.

~

You don't need to be much of a musician to toot your own horn.

~

Before you start a speech, you should say something.

~

Teach your children the value of a dollar. Give them a dime.

~

Poverty never drives a man to drink, but drink will drive a man to poverty.

~

True progress is to balance our wants to present income.

~

To disagree, one does not have to be disagreeable.

~

Instead of putting others in their place, put yourself in their place.

~

It's not only what you pay a fellow but what he costs you that counts.

~

About the hardest thing to replace after it is worn out is a welcome.

~

The problem with the human race is that it has such low admission standards.

~

A man isn't actually poor if he can still laugh.

~

The impersonal hand of government can never replace the helping hand of a neighbor.

~

There are two ways of being rich. One is to have all you want; the other is to be satisfied with what you have.

~

While searching for riches, don't lose the things that money can't buy. It is what we value, not what we have, that really makes us rich.

~

If you talk about yourself, you're a bore. If you talk about others, you're a gossip.

~

There are two types of people who say very little — the quiet ones and the gabby ones.

∼

Blessed is the man who is too busy to worry in the daytime and too sleepy to worry at night.

∼

Why worry about things that never happen? Worries are mostly about yesterday and tomorrow.

∼

Fat around the waist, though not desired, is better than fat between the ears.

∼

Knowledge becomes wisdom only after it has been put to practical use.

∼

A fool and his money never appear when you need a loan.

∼

Great opportunities come to those who make the most of small opportunities.

∼

Worry is wasting today's time to clutter up tomorrow's opportunities with yesterday's troubles.

∼

If you want to soar with the eagles in the morning, you can't hoot with the owls at night.

∼

If you think your jobs are small and the rewards are few, just remember that the mighty oak was once a nut like you.

∼

Ideas not put into practice are merely dreams.

∼

Most of us get what we deserve, but only the successful person will admit it.

∼

How long a minute is depends on which side of the bathroom door you're on.

∼

People with patience put up with people they'd rather put down.

∼

If we don't improve our schools, every child in America will get a free education — free of any knowledge whatsoever.

∼

Money can't buy happiness, but it lets you look in the best places.

≈

Speeches should be like women's skirts — just long enough to cover the subject and short enough to create interest.

≈

Sleep late. The early birds get worms.

≈

Don't be afraid of tomorrow because when it comes, it will be today.

≈

If folks didn't carry gossip, it wouldn't go so far.

≈

A yard without a tree is not fit for a dog.

≈

The jawbone of an ass is just as dangerous today as it was in Samson's time.

≈

Experience is sometimes a very costly commodity that rarely has resale value.

≈

A sure way to stop a hot argument is to lay a few cold facts on it.

≈

The function of fear is merely to warn us of danger.

≈

More painful than acting foolish is to suddenly realize you're not acting.

≈

A practical gift is one you can afford.

≈

A small house will hold as much happiness as a large one.

≈

Appreciation is always appreciated.

≈

Anybody who thinks money is everything has never been sick.

≈

Reasons that sound good and good, sound reasons may be quite different.

≈

Quiet people are not the only ones who don't say much.

~

The best way to take the wind out of an angry person's sails is to stay calm.

~

Temper is a weak man's imitation of strength.

~

The most efficient water power in the world is women's tears.

~

When it comes to giving, some people stop at nothing.

~

Influence is a thing you think you have until you try to use it.

~

Women cannot be as successful in business as men because they have no wives to advise them.

~

The fellow who keeps his head while all those around him are losing theirs will be a head taller.

~

Nobody needs a smile as much as he who has none to give.

~

In some restaurants the best waiters are the customers.

~

Kindness is a language that the deaf can hear and the blind can see.

~

When the going seems easy, check to make sure you're not going downhill.

~

The darkest hour has but sixty minutes.

~

It takes a magician to pull a rabbit out of a hat, but most any fool can let the cat out of the bag.

~

The best thing you can spend on your children is time.

~

Don't spend your time the way politicians spend our money.

～

Making time count is more important than counting time.

～

Time is like money. You can only spend it once.

～

Laughter is a shock absorber that eases the blows of life.

～

The best security blanket a child can have is parents who love each other.

～

Life is like a mechanical pencil. You can't make your mark unless you get the lead out.

～

If a young boy being given a bath turns red, the water is too hot; if he turns blue, the water is too cold; if he turns white, he needed a bath.

～

Life is like riding a bicycle. You don't fall off unless you stop pedaling.

～

Many people would see better days if they didn't run around all night.

～

To avoid criticism, do nothing, say nothing, be nothing.

～

It is extremely difficult for a child to live right if he has never seen it done.

～

Laughter translates into any language.

～

This will be a much better world when the power of love replaces the love of power.

～

A hypocrite prays on his knees on Sunday and preys on his neighbors the rest of the week.

～

Don't miss the good things that money can't buy.

～

Rejecting things because they are old-fashioned would rule out the sun, moon and a mother's love.

~

Why don't people jump at opportunities as quickly as they jump to conclusions?

~

Prejudice is a great time saver. It enables you to form opinions without bothering to get the facts.

~

The frightening thing about heredity and environment is that parents provide both.

~

Experience is what tells you to watch your step, and is also what you'll get if you don't watch your step.

~

Humor is to life what shock absorbers are to automobiles.

~

The right train of thought can take you to a better station in life.

~

I heard of a couple who is in the iron and steel business. She irons and he steals.

~

Things always turn out best for the fellow who makes the best of how things turn out.

~

What difference will a specific decision make in ten years?

~

I don't see the harm in letting children believe in Santa Claus, but more of them should be told the facts of life before they become voting age.

~

Happiness is a healthy mental attitude, a grateful spirit, a clear conscience and a heart full of love.

~

Experience is knowing a lot of things you shouldn't do.

~

Common sense combined with the Golden Rule could produce a fair amount of good luck. You may have to add some carefully executed good planning.

~

Life is really simple. We ourselves create the circumstances that complicate life.

~

Many of us go through life not knowing what we want, but feeling sure we don't have it.

~

A task worth doing and friends worth having make life worthwhile.

~

The tragedy of life is not that it ends too soon, but that we wait so long to begin it.

~

The trouble with life is that you're halfway through it before you realize it's one of those do-it-yourself deals.

~

As we go down life's highway, many of us now wish we had consulted a travel agent first.

~

Laughter is a tranquilizer and carries no side effects.

~

Contentment in life consists not in great wealth but in simple wants.

~

Start living to beat hell.

~

Worth remembering: The value of time; the success of perseverance; the dignity of simplicity; the worth of character; the virtue of patience; the wisdom of economy; the power of kindness.

~

Experience may not be worth what it costs but we can't seem to get it for any less.

~

Good humor is the health of the soul.

~

It seldom occurs to teenagers that someday they will know as little as their parents do today.

You can't measure happiness by the amount of money a person has. A person with ten million dollars may be no happier than one with only nine million.

~

A sign of a child growing up is when he stops asking where he came from and doesn't tell you where he is going.

～

Good advice on raising children is to enjoy them while they're still on your side.

～

In Hollywood, if you don't have a psychiatrist, people think you're crazy.

～

Life is sort of a do-it-yourself kit. Be sure your parts fit into the scheme of things.

～

In the old days, that house would have burned to the ground in half an hour. Now, with all the modern equipment, the firemen managed to keep the fire going all day.

～

Children act like their parents in spite of every effort to teach them good manners.

～

Women make fools of some men. Other men are the do-it-yourself type.

～

Many family trees have a shady branch.

～

Family trees seem to produce a large variety of nuts.

～

Every day, do something to make other people happy — even if it's only to leave them alone.

～

Wealth does not insure happiness; neither does poverty. Happiness will never come to those who fail to appreciate what they already have.

～

With proper care, the human body will last a lifetime.

～

Life is like playing a slot machine. You can't hit the jackpot without putting something in it.

～

Living life to its fullest does not mean overeating.

～

Many fathers should worry less about their golf swing and more about their offspring.

～

Life insurance keeps you poor all your life so you can die rich.

~

Maybe all children could keep on the straight and narrow path if they knew someone who's been over the route and could inform them.

~

No wonder there are juvenile delinquents. Mama is busy keeping up with the Joneses, and papa is so busy keeping up with mama that neither of them has time left for keeping up with John and Mary.

~

Having teenagers is often what undermines a parent's belief in heredity.

~

Father: "My hardest job is getting my son to realize 'No' is a complete sentence."

~

Usually it's the father who is working his son through college.

~

Just think how little our parents knew about child psychology and how wonderful we turned out.

~

Every time you graduate from the school of experience, someone thinks up a new course.

~

Four and seventeen are the most desirable ages. At four, you know all the questions; at seventeen, you know all the answers.

~

Life's greatest satisfactions include getting the last laugh, having the last word and paying the last installment.

~

It is difficult for a child to live right if he has never seen it done.

~

A pat on the back will develop character if given low enough, often enough, young enough and hard enough.

~

Commencement is when the college students who learned all the answers discover that there is a new set of questions.

~

Child training is chiefly a matter of knowing which end of the child to pat — and when.

～

A modern home is a place where a switch controls everything except the children.

～

Many a juvenile delinquent is a youngster who has been given a free hand, but not in the proper place.

～

Warm hearts and cool heads maintain the right temperature in a home.

～

Do it now! Today will be yesterday tomorrow.

～

Now there is one politically mixed up family — the wife is a republican, the husband is a democrat, the kids are wet, the cow is dry and the cat is on the fence.

～

Modern children who run away from home may be looking for their parents.

～

The behavior of some children suggests that their parents embarked on the sea of matrimony without a paddle.

～

Alcoholics in a small town are seldom anonymous.

～

A babysitter used to be called mother.

～

Weigh your neighbor in the same balance with yourself.

～

People don't usually make the same mistake twice — it's usually three or four times.

～

How to be happy: Keep your heart free from hate, your mind free from worry, live simply, expect little, give much, sing often, pray always, forget yourself, think of others and their feelings, fill your heart with love, scatter sunshine. These are tried links in the golden chain of contentment.

~

Most people do not realize the impact of attitude on life. Attitude is more important than money, circumstances, failures, successes or skills. It will make or break a company, a church, or any endeavor. We all have a choice every day regarding attitude that we will embrace for that specific day. We cannot change our past. We cannot change how people will react to certain things. The only thing we can play on is our attitude. I read that life is ten percent what happens to us and ninety percent how we react to it.

~

Two fellows went hunting. One told his newfound friend that he was known to snore at night, and if he did hear him snoring he should simply get up and shake him. Shortly after they turned out the lights, his buddy came over to his bunk and kissed him on the cheek. There was no more snoring that night.

~

Conversation between two small boys in the children's ward of a hospital:
First boy: "Are you medical or surgical?"
Second boy: "I don't know what you mean by that."
First boy: "Well, were you sick when you came in, or did they make you sick after you got here?"

~

How to Measure Man:
- ▲ Not — how did he die? But — how did he live?
- ▲ Not — what did he gain? But — what did he give?
- ▲ Not — what was his station? But — did he have heart?
- ▲ Not — what was his church or creed? But — did he befriend those in need?
- ▲ Not — what did his obituary read? But — how many were sorry when he passed away?

~

Sophie: "My father is a model man. He doesn't drink, he doesn't smoke, he never runs around with other women, he doesn't go to shows. In fact, he has no vices and he is going to celebrate his eightieth birthday tomorrow."
Clifford: "How?"

∾

You are richer today than you were yesterday if you have laughed often, given something, forgiven even more, made a new friend, made stepping stones of stumbling blocks, or if you have managed to be cheerful even if you were weary.

∾

You can tell it's going to be a rotten day when:
- ▲ You wake up face down on the sidewalk.
- ▲ You come to work and find a "60 Minutes" news team waiting at your office.
- ▲ Your birthday cake collapses from the weight of the candles.
- ▲ You want to launder the clothes you wore home from the party last night and they aren't there.
- ▲ You turn on the TV news and they're showing emergency routes out of the city.
- ▲ You stop at the post office on a holiday and bump your nose on the locked door.
- ▲ You wake up and discover your waterbed broke, and then you realize that you don't have a waterbed.
- ▲ Your car horn sticks as you follow a group of Hell's Angels on the freeway.
- ▲ Your boss tells you not to bother to take off your coat.
- ▲ The bird singing outside your window turns out to be a buzzard.
- ▲ You call your answering service and they tell you it's none of your business.
- ▲ Your income tax refund check bounces.
- ▲ You put both contact lenses in the same eye.
- ▲ Your wife says, "Good morning, Bill," and your name is George.

∾

A few things wrong with the world today:

▲ Not enough honest leaders of people.

▲ Too many chasers of women.

▲ Too many fall down on their duties.

▲ Too much love of power.

▲ Not enough people concerned about the future or willing to prepare for it.

∾

Both the hummingbird and the vulture fly over our nation's deserts. All that the vulture sees is rotting meat, because that is what it is looking for. It thrives on that diet. The hummingbird looks for colorful blossoms of desert plants. It fills itself with the freshness of life. Each bird finds what it is looking for. We do, too.

∾

TEN COMMANDMENTS OF HUMAN RELATIONS

1. Speak to people. There is nothing so nice as a cheerful greeting.

2. Smile at people. It takes more muscles to frown than to smile.

3. Call people by name. It is music to anyone's ears to hear their own name.

4. Be friendly. To have friends, you need to be one.

5. Be genial. Speak and act as if everything you do is a pleasure.

6. Be genuinely interested. People want to know that you care about what they say.

7. Praise generously. This is uplifting to a person. Be careful when you criticize.

8. Be considerate. Feelings can be hurt rather easily. Don't be rude even when you disagree.

9. Give service. It's more fun to give than to receive. You'll make somebody's day.

10. Add to these a sense of humor, patience and humility, and you will be rewarded.

FAITH & RELIGION

Too many adults and not enough children believe in Santa Claus.

～

Let us pray, not for lighter burdens, but for stronger backs.

～

Don't pray for more material things than you are willing to work for.

～

Don't pray for an easy life. Pray to be a stronger person.

～

Good judgment should be used prior to judgment day.

～

God does answer prayers. Sometimes we don't like the answers.

～

A person who looks up to God rarely looks down on any person.

～

Let us all make our blessings count as well as counting our blessings.

～

Soft soap in the pulpit will not cleanse the sinners in the pew.

～

God gives us the ingredients for our daily bread, but he expects us to do the baking.

～

We keep asking God to bless America. He already has. Now it's our turn.

～

After saying our prayers, we ought to do something to make them come true.

～

God sends food for every bird but he doesn't put the food in their nest.

～

Prayers usually don't work when we ask God to run errands for us. Ask God for a change in character and not for a change in circumstances.

～

The Christ child was one who knew more than his parents did, yet he obeyed them.

～

A good Christian is one who makes it easier for other people to believe in God.

～

Sign in a high school building: In the event of an earthquake or tornado, the Supreme Court ruling against prayer in school will be temporarily suspended.

~

Prayer must not be taken out of public schools. That's the only way many of us got through school.

~

A long life is a gift of God. A full and fruitful life is your own doing.

~

Life is fragile; handle with prayer.

~

There are a lot of Christians who haven't stored up enough treasures to make a down payment on a harp.

~

Be sure you know who's knocking — opportunity or temptation.

~

Get ready for eternity. You're going to spend a lot of time there.

~

Discouraged? Try praying.

~

If people did not sin, churches would not have much business.

~

In the Bible, we read about Jonah and the whale. Said story precisely tells us that "you can't keep a good man down."

~

Noah was the first businessman mentioned in the Bible. He floated a company at a time when the rest of the world was under liquidation.

~

Noah took two of each kind of animal into the ark because he didn't believe the story about the stork.

~

If you want to go to heaven, turn right and keep going straight.

~

If the good Lord had intended for us to live in a permissive society the Ten Commandments would have been called the Ten Suggestions.

~

The Lord sometimes takes us into troubled waters, not to drown us but to cleanse us.

～

After two thousand years, our church is still under the same management.

～

An atheist has no one to talk to when alone.

～

Everybody should listen to a good sermon occasionally, especially the people who got to church.

～

The highest reward that God gives us is the ability to do better.

～

You should read the Bible more frequently, then you won't have to do so much cramming for your finals later.

～

Noah must have been an optimist. He took two (male and female) termites on a wooden boat.

～

Everyone wants to go to heaven, but no one wants to die.

～

Most of us would have more trouble than we have if all our prayers had been answered.

～

The pastor stopped in the middle of his sermon. "Clara, would you please wake up Jack?" Clara replied, "You wake him up, you put him to sleep."

～

If all the people that sleep in church were laid end to end, they would be much more comfortable.

～

Dad criticized the sermon, mother thought the organist made a lot of mistakes, sister didn't like the choir's singing. But they all shut up when Little Sven said, "Still it was a pretty good show for a quarter."

～

While flying in a violent thunderstorm, everyone on the plane was looking to the only clergyman on board for comfort. "Can you do something?"

"I'm sorry," said the reverend gently. "I'm in sales, not in management."

～

Pastor: "A mule died in front of our church."
Deacon: "Well, it's the job of the ministers to look after the dead. Why tell me?"
Pastor: "You're right, it's my job. But we always notify the next of kin."

∾

Pastor showing the church building to a prospective member: "Here is a plaque for men who died in the service."
Prospect: "Which service — morning or evening?"

∾

A pastor was invited for dinner and was asked to lead the prayer before the meal. After a brief prayer, little Kirsten said approvingly, "You don't pray so long when you're hungry."

∾

Little girl telling the story of Adam and Eve: "First God created Adam. Then He looked at him and said, 'I think I can do better if I tried again.'"

∾

Adam and Eve were the first gamblers. Then God took their pair o' dice away from them.

∾

If Adam would come back to earth today, the only thing he would still recognize is the jokes.

∾

Adam was rejected for Eden the apple.

∾

A pastor was concentrating on his sermon and cut himself while shaving. A member suggested that he concentrate on his shaving and cut his sermon.

∾

Mother: "Henry, little Billy swallowed a coin."
Father: "Call our minister. He can get money out of anybody."

∾

Priest: "Rabbi, when are you going to break down and eat ham?"
Rabbi: "At your wedding, Father."

∾

Church member: "Pastor, your sermon was very instructive. You know, we really didn't know what sin was until you came here."

∾

We had a membership drive in our church. Last week we drove off thirty-five.

~

The first Adam-splitting gave us Eve, a force which ingenious men of all ages have never fully gotten under control.

~

The children's sermon subject was describing how Lot's wife looked back and suddenly turned into a pillar of salt. Little Johnny contributed, "My mother looked back once while driving our car and turned into a telephone pole."

~

When Eve tried to get out of the Garden of Eden without him, Adam called the commanding officer: "Eve is absent without leaf."

~

Eve: "Adam, do you still love me?"
Adam: "Who else?"

~

A pastor during a children's sermon talked about the burnt offerings written about in the Old Testament. "Why don't we have burnt offerings today?"
Young boy: "On account of air pollution."

~

An atheist is a disbeliever who prefers to raise his children in a Christian community.

~

Sign on the tombstone of an atheist: Here lies an atheist, all dressed up and no place to go.

~

Visitor: "Pastor, how many of your members are active?"
Pastor: "They all are! Some are active for the Lord and some are active for the devil."

~

The reason God made woman after He made man was because He didn't want any advice.

~

Don't be afraid to trust an unknown future to a well-known God.

~

An evangelist recently announced there are seven hundred and twenty-seven sins. I understand he is getting requests for that list from people who think they might be missing something.

~

Faith is the quality that enables you to eat blackberry jam on a picnic without looking to see whether the seeds are moving.

~

Attending church services regularly does not necessarily mean one attends church religiously.

~

The world does not need a definition of religion as much as it needs a demonstration.

~

There are people practicing religion today but not enough are good at it.

~

If your religion can easily be hidden, it can easily be lost.

~

I'm sure that preacher didn't carry his sermon around in a briefcase.

~

If a sermon pricks the conscience, it must have good points.

~

A poor listener seldom hears a good sermon.

~

On preaching a funeral sermon, a preacher said, "We have here before us only the shell. The nut is gone."

~

Our church serves coffee after the sermon — presumably to awaken everyone before they start driving home.

~

Prayer must mean something to us if it is to mean anything to God.

~

Satan has no unemployment problems.

~

The reason many sermons seem dull is because preachers often try to answer questions that nobody is asking.

~

Prayer for a modern youth: "Lord, lead us not into temptation. Just tell us where it is and we'll find it."

~

I pity the pastor who bought a used car and didn't have the vocabulary to make it run.

〜

〜

"This morning," said the minister to his congregation, "I'm going to speak on the relationship between fact and faith. It is a fact that you are sitting here in the sanctuary. It is also a fact that I am standing here speaking. But it is faith that makes me believe that you might be listening to what I have to say."

〜

Roland: "I was born a Lutheran, I've always been a Lutheran, and I'll die a Lutheran. No one is going to make a Christian out of me."

〜

A group of preachers recently formed a bowling league. They call themselves the Holy Rollers.

〜

A preacher comforts the afflicted and afflicts the comfortable.

〜

Little Ole started Sunday school. At the first session, the teacher showed the youngsters a picture of the Christians being thrown to the lions. Then the teacher saw little Ole crying, so she asked him, "What is the matter?"

"That one poor lion," sobbed Ole, "he ain't got no Christian."

A five-year-old boy came home from school in tears. He told his mother that the teacher had asked all those who wanted to go to heaven to raise their hands. The mother said, "You raised your hand, didn't you?"

"No," said the boy. "You told me to come straight home."

〜

Preacher: "Remember, my son, we are in the world to help others."

Young boy: "What are the others here for?"

〜

In heaven everyone has wings. In hell, they travel by helicopter.

〜

He has his religion in his wife's name.

〜

The sermon topic was "gossip" followed by the hymn "I love to tell a story."

〜

Work for the Lord. The pay isn't much but the retirement plan is out of this world.

〜

"Do you really believe," asked the atheist, "that Jonah spent three days and nights in the belly of a whale?"

"I don't know," replied the Salvation Army lass, "but I'll ask him when I get to heaven."

"But suppose he isn't there," said the atheist.

Quickly came the reply, "Then you can ask him."

≈

Pastor: "My mission in life is to save men."

Lulu: "Save one for me."

≈

Our Lord is in the cleansing business, not in the whitewashing business.

≈

People give to their church until it hurts. Some people are more sensitive to pain than others.

≈

Usher in church: "Sleeping or non-sleeping section?"

≈

Support the church with your money. You can't take it with you, but you can send it ahead.

≈

If everybody obeyed the Ten Commandments, we would have a scarcity of news.

≈

A young boy's prayer: "Lord, if you can't make me a better boy, don't worry about it. I'm having a good time as it is."

≈

Our preachers are called to be shepherds, not sheep dogs.

≈

Is it poor preaching in our pulpits or is it poor praying in the pew?

≈

The devil called St. Peter and asked him to get the Lutheran pastor and the Catholic priest out of hell. "Between bingo and lutefisk, they are killing the other businesses down here."

≈

Father: "Son, did you learn anything new in Sunday school today?"

Son: "We sure did. I learned all about a cross-eyed bear named Gladly. We even sang a song, 'Gladly the Cross I'd Bear.'"

≈

The sermon topic was liquor: "All the liquor should be thrown into the river." The church service concluded by singing, "Shall we gather at the river?"

~

Men need faith that will not shrink when washed in waters of affliction and adversity.

~

Read your Bible. A chapter a day keeps Satan away.

~

A religion not strong enough to take you to church services on Sunday may not take you to heaven when you die.

~

A bishop was walking along a street when he saw a little girl trying to reach a doorbell. The bishop rang the doorbell for her. "Thanks," she said, "now run like hell."

~

Teacher: "Those who tell lies don't go to heaven."
Little Ole: "It must be very lonely up there with only God and George Washington."

~

If your troubles are deep-seated and longstanding, try kneeling.

~

Pastor: "What must we do to get forgiveness for our sins?"
Kirsten: "We must commit them first."

~

A Catholic boy said to a Jewish boy, "Our parish priest knows much more than your rabbi." The Jewish boy said, "He should, you tell him everything."

~

Drive carefully. Remember it's not only the car that can be recalled by its maker.

~

Sunday school teacher: "Why in your prayer do you only ask for your daily bread instead of asking for a week's supply?"
Little Ole: "So we can get it fresh every day."

~

The teacher held up a picture to her class of Jesus riding into Jerusalem on the first Palm Sunday. A little boy said to his friend, "Hasn't he grown a lot since Christmas?"

～

Grandma mailing the family Bible to her grandson:
Postal clerk: "Does this package contain anything valuable?"
Grandma: "Yes, the Ten Commandments."

～

If people would spend as much energy practicing their religion as they do quarreling about it, what a great world this would be.

～

Sunday school teacher: "God lives in heaven, is that correct, Johnny?"
Johnny: "No ma'am. He lives in the bathroom at our house."
Teacher: "The bathroom?"
Johnny: "Every morning, my dad stands outside the door and shouts, 'My God, are you still in there?'"

～

We must distinguish between childish faith and child-like faith.

～

Missionary: "Poor man, so you know nothing of religion?"
Cannibal: "Oh, yes, I got a taste of it when the last missionary was here."

～

A preacher once remarked to his congregation that every blade of grass was a sermon. A few days later while the preacher was mowing his lawn, a witty member passed by and remarked, "That's right, pastor, cut your sermons short."

～

Adam and Eve invented the loose leaf system.

～

The number one Bible salesman in the entire United States of America was called in by the publishing company to speak at a seminar. The emcee introduced the star sales-person and instructed him to give his sales pitch as follows: "Assuming you just rang the doorbell and the homeowner came to the door. You start your sales presentation."
"Hel-lo, do yu-yu-yu you wa-wa-wa want to bi-bi-bi-buy a bi-bi-Bible? O-o-o-or sh-sh-should I re-re-re-read it to you?"

～

Ole and Sven were walking down the road and came upon a dead animal. Ole said, "It's a mule." Sven said, "It's a donkey." Finally the minister came along. "Pastor, what is this?" they asked. The minister assured them that it was an ass. Coming from the minister, both accepted the fact that it was an ass and proceeded to bury the animal. Lena came by and asked, "Are you digging a foxhole?" Ole replied, "No, not according to the scriptures."

≈

A preacher was called to substitute for the regular minister. The speaker began by explaining the meaning of a substitute. "If you break a window and then place a piece of cardboard there, that is a substitute." After the sermon, a woman who had listened intently shook his hand and wishing to compliment him said, "You were not a substitute. You were a real pane."

≈

A real estate loan officer died. Since the loan officer lived a decent life, St. Peter decided to give him a choice. St. Peter opened a door to heaven to give the loan officer a good look. Everything was beautiful and quiet. After that demonstration, St. Peter opened the door to hell, for the loan officer to examine. Here he saw a big party, pretty girls, dancing, music, etc. That looked good to the loan officer, even though he had been a conservative loan officer all his life and had heard such wonderful things about heaven. This made it hard to make a decision. "I'll give you my answer tomorrow," the loan officer said. The following day, the loan officer told St. Peter, "I have decided to go to hell." St. Peter opened the door to hell to have him enter. The loan officer saw fire and smoke and heard crying and moaning. The loan officer said, "This is not what you showed me yesterday!" St. Peter replied, "You should have locked in yesterday."

≈

Ole and Lena went to a revival meeting where an evangelist was conducting a very emotional service. Working up to a fever pitch, the preacher exhorted the crowd: "All of you who want to go to heaven, step forward. Come up to the altar." Everyone came forward except Ole and Lena. The evangelist noticed the holdouts and asked, "Don't you want to go to heaven?"
"Sure we do," answered Ole, "but we didn't know you were getting up a load to go right now."

~

A Baptist minister arrived in a small town to preach a sermon. Wanting to mail a letter, he asked a young boy where the post office was. After the boy told him, the minister invited the boy to the Baptist church that evening, saying, "You can hear me telling everyone how to get to heaven."

"I don't think I'll be there," said the boy. "You don't even know your way to the post office."

~

A politician, a surgeon and an engineer were arguing over whose profession was the first one to be established. "Mine is," said the surgeon. "The Bible says that Eve was created by excising a rib from Adam."

"But before that," said the engineer, "a six-day engineering job created the earth out of utter chaos."

"Aha," said the politician, "but who created the chaos?"

~

Easter story: Ole, Sven and Pat died simultaneously. The three were walking up the narrow path when St. Peter intercepted them. "You fellows may not go beyond this point until each one can tell me what Easter is all about. Ole, you tell me about Easter."

Ole: "Easter is when you bake a large turkey, pumpkin pie, cranberries, sweet potatoes..."

"No, no," replied St. Peter. "Sven, you tell me about Easter."

Sven: "Easter is when you have a decorated tree in the house, buy a lot of gifts..."

"No, no," said St. Peter. "Now, Pat, you tell us about Easter."

Pat: "Easter is when the people crucified a man named Jesus. After Jesus was dead, they buried him in a tomb and rolled a large rock over the door. Three days later, Jesus got up, rolled the rock away..."

St. Peter interrupted. "Ole, Sven, you two listen to Pat. Proceed, Pat."

Pat: "After three days Jesus got up, rolled the large stone away from the door, walked outside and saw his shadow."

~

A young man who worked at a lumber company took home a piece of lumber every evening after work. Soon he had a large pile of lumber. Finally, his conscience began to bother him. Being Catholic, he went to see his priest and confessed everything. Father listened very intently and then said, "Young man, you have done something very, very serious. You must make a novena. Do you know what a novena is?"

"No, Father," he said, "I don't, but if you have plans, I've got the lumber."

~

A preacher forgot his notes for the sermon. In the midst of the sermon, he got a few things twisted when he said, "The Lord took four thousand barley loaves and six thousand fish and fed twenty-four people, and had much food left over." Someone in the congregation called out, "Anybody could do that." After the service when the minister complained about the heckler, he was told of his error by a deacon. The next week the minister stepped forward confidently with notes of his sermon in hand. In the course of his sermon, he again brought up the miracle of the loaves and fish. He told how the five barley loaves and the two fish had fed the multitude of approximately 24,000 people. Then he pointed to the heckler from the previous Sunday and asked, "Could you do that?"

"I sure could," said the heckler.

"And just how would you do that?" asked the minister.

"With the loaves and fish left over from last Sunday."

FRIENDSHIP, LOVE
& MARRIAGE

Friends last much longer if you don't use them much.

~

A friend is a present you give to yourself.

~

If a fellow can't say nice things about his friends, he ought to get some new friends.

~

It's smart to pick a friend, but not to pieces.

~

A friend you can buy can be bought from you.

~

You can't cultivate friends by digging up dirt around them.

~

Promises may get friends, but it is performance that keeps them.

~

This will be a better world when the power of love replaces the love of power.

~

A friend is someone who makes you feel totally acceptable.

~

A friend is some one who knows all about you and still loves you.

~

The best antique is an old friend.

~

Don't bore your friends with your troubles. Tell your troubles to your enemies. They'll be delighted to hear about them.

~

You can't keep your friends by giving them away.

~

Ole says it's foolish for folks to be spending so much time loving their enemies when they could be treating their friends a little better.

~

A friend who is not in need is a friend indeed.

~

To have a friend, be a friend.

~

Real friends are those who, when you've made a fool of yourself, don't feel that you've done a permanent job. They warm you by their presence, trust you with their secrets and remember you in their prayers.

～

A real friend will tell you your faults and follies in times of prosperity, and assist you with his hand and heart in times of adversity.

～

When you lend money to a friend, you may damage his memory.

～

We are all to love our neighbors as we do ourselves — but could they stand that much affection?

～

This will be a better world when the power of love replaces the love of power.

～

The more perfect a man is, the more the girls try to altar him.

～

The first domestic dispute was when Eve kept putting Adam's pants in the salad by mistake.

～

A good friend of mine had a good education, worked hard, saved his money, and became wealthy when he married a rich widow.

～

A man doesn't know the value of a woman's love until he starts paying alimony.

～

When people get married for better or worse, they mean they can't do better and may do worse.

～

Fifty percent of all marriages end in divorce, but a hundred percent of all divorces begin with marriage.

～

No woman makes a fool out of a man - she merely directs the performance.

～

The best time to do the dishes is right after your wife tells you to.

～

The penalty for bigamy is two mothers-in law.

～

Many women don't live up to their marriage vows. Both parties take an oath to grow old together and then she has her husband go ahead without her.

~

When our spouse is no longer suspicious when we come home late, it may be later than we think.

~

A father is one who is forced to endure childbirth without an anesthetic.

~

A good friend of mine had a good education, worked hard, saved his money, and became wealthy when he married a rich widow.

~

Tomorrow my neighbor is taking his wife to a beauty parlor for an estimate.

~

A married couple should save each other for old age.

~

When a husband says he can't do something due to circumstances beyond his control, he means his wife won't let him.

~

Lee is getting married. He got hooked by his own line.

~

A marriage license, like a fishing or hunting license, does not guarantee a prize catch.

~

King Solomon was a great man. Any man who can manage a thousand wives deserves to be remembered.

~

A good wife laughs at her husband's jokes, not because they are clever but because she is.

~

Statistics show that men who kiss their wives good-bye in the morning live six years longer than those who don't. You guys should pucker up before you tucker out.

~

The average woman remembers when and where she got married. What escapes her is why.

~

Some people marry for money, some for love, and others for a short time.

〜

Mrs. Gossip: "So your daughter is about to marry. Do you really feel she is ready for the battle of life?"
Mrs. Chatter: "She's been in four engagements already."

〜

We've had adult education for several thousand years. It's called marriage.

〜

Sophie: "Before we were married, you told me that you were well off."
Clifford: "I was, but I didn't know it."

〜

Roland: "I want a divorce. My wife hasn't spoken to me in six months."
Attorney: "You better keep her, you'll never find another woman like her."

〜

Ella: "When I first met my husband, it was obvious he was nobody's fool. So I decided he might as well be mine."

〜

The beatnik girl got married. Instead of giving her a shower, they made her take one.

〜

"I don't like marriage. Joe hasn't kissed me since the honeymoon."
"Why don't you divorce Joe?"
"I can't, I married Bill."

〜

Who introduced you to your husband?
We just met. I don't blame anyone.

〜

Wife: "I was a fool when I married you."
Husband: "I know, but I was so infatuated with you at the time, I didn't notice."

〜

Every woman has a mental picture of the man she wants to marry, and if she doesn't get the one she wants, heaven help the one she gets.

〜

Lulu is a good housekeeper. Every time she gets a divorce, she keeps the house.

〜

A thoughtful husband will leave the lawn mower and garden tools where his wife can find them easily.

〜

A husband is a man who lost his liberty in the pursuit of happiness.

～

Husband to wife: "Sure you may have that fur coat. Who offered you one, dear?"

～

Two women were consoling each other — one had lost her husband to another woman. The other was the woman who got him.

～

Herb: "They tell me your wife is outspoken."
Alex: "By whom?"

～

Attendant: "Doctor, there is a man outside who wants to know if we've lost any of our men from the insane asylum."
Doctor: "Why is that?"
Attendant: "He says that someone has run off with his wife."

～

Ole and Lena had a little quarrel while driving down a country road. Lena spotted a jackass grazing along the road and asked Ole, "Is that a relative of yours?"
"Of course," said Ole, "by marriage."

～

Joan: "I simply can't stand my husband. He has such a nasty disposition. He's made me so jittery that I'm losing weight."
Mother: "Why don't you leave him and come back home?"
Joan: "Oh, I will. I'm just waiting until he gets me down to a hundred and twenty pounds."

～

Wife telling her husband: "I was just as unreasonable before we were married, dear, only then you thought it was cute."

～

They would make a perfect couple. He's a pill and she's a headache.

～

Sam: "What makes you think that your wife is getting tired of you?"
Leo: "All this week she's been wrapping my lunch in a road map."

～

A woman is orderly by nature, but it's a mistake for her to always put her husband in his place.

～

Wife to husband: "When I want your opinion, I'll give it to you."

∾

Gus: "Does your wife pick your suits?"
Andy: "No, just my pockets."

∾

"Every time you talk, you say my house, my automobile, my chair, my shoes — everything is yours. You never say ours. I'm your partner. I'm your wife. It should be ours." The husband kept looking around the room. "What are you looking for," the wife asked. "I'm looking for our pants."

∾

I promised my wife a mink for her birthday if she would keep the cage clean.

∾

Wife: "I'm afraid the mountain air would disagree with me."
Husband: "My dear, it wouldn't dare."

∾

Tom: "If a wedding means showers for the bride, what does it mean for the groom?"
Jerry: "Curtains."

∾

"My wife always has the last word."
"You're lucky. Mine never gets to it."

∾

Lulu: "My pastor said we could have sixteen husbands."
Sophie: "That's not right."
Lulu: "Yes, at the last wedding at our church I heard him say, 'four better, four worse, four richer, four poorer.'"

∾

A woman offered a brand new Porsche for sale for a price of ten dollars. A man answered the ad, but was disbelieving. "What's the gimmick," he inquired.
"No gimmick," the woman answered. "My husband died and in his will he asked that the car be sold and all proceeds given to his secretary."

∾

Boy: "Will you marry me?"
Girl: "No, but I'll always admire your good taste."

∾

Policeman: "How did this accident happen?"
Motorist: "My wife fell asleep in the back seat."

~

A definition of the word widow as given by a little boy to his teacher: A widow is a woman who lived with her husband so long that he died.

~

If a man has a wife, it is not possible for him to make a fool of himself and not know it.

~

Judge: "You cannot get a divorce merely because your husband has flat feet."
Lady: "Not flat feet — feet in the wrong flat."

~

Successful man: One who earns more than his wife can spend.

~

Successful woman: One who finds such a man.

~

Some girls win husbands by exhibiting generous natures; others by exhibiting how generous nature has been to them.

~

Jack and Jill divorced for health reasons. They got sick of each other.

~

A girl was asked what she desired most in a husband — brains, wealth or appearance. "Appearance," she replied, "and the sooner the better."

~

Some widows get rid of the darkness in their lives by striking another match.

~

Ella: "Your husband's a card among the cuties."
Maggie: "The trouble is, he wants to shuffle the whole deck."

~

Lulu: "If I could combine their qualities, I'd be the happiest girl in the world. Lester is cute, debonair and rich, witty and handsome, and Roland wants to marry me."

~

A radio station doing a survey phoned one thousand men and asked them, "Who are you listening to?" Ninety-seven percent were listening to their wives.

~

When a woman smiles at her husband the way she smiles at a traffic cop, you know she loves her husband.

~

If at first you don't succeed, try doing it the way your wife told you.

~

I noticed a newlywed squeezing a can of soup to see if it was fresh.

~

A sure way to save a marriage from divorce is not to show up for the wedding.

~

There was a good girl who had been saying no so long that she almost loused up her wedding ceremony.

~

In spite of all the plans for world peace, why do we have the usual number of weddings?

~

A tenth wedding anniversary is difficult to celebrate. It's too soon to brag and too late to complain.

~

The wedding is a ceremony where the bridegroom starts kissing the bride and the other fellows stop.

~

According to police records, no wife ever shot her husband while he was doing the dishes.

~

An ex-wife is more expensive than a wife.

~

A sure way to support a wife in the manner to which she's accustomed is to have her keep her job.

~

The ideal wife is one who sits up with you when you're sick and puts up with you when you're not.

~

Some women take a man for better or for worse; others for all he has.

~

A model wife is one who, when she spades the garden, picks up the fish worms for her husband.

~

Many modern day brides have not been kitchen tested.

~

A perfect wife is one who does not expect a perfect husband.

∾

A man who doesn't know what his wife is thinking has not been listening.

∾

A smart wife sees through her husband; a good wife sees him through.

∾

Some wives hire private detectives to find out why their husbands are so happy.

∾

If a woman can be a sweetheart, valet, audience, cook and a nurse, she is qualified for marriage.

∾

A loving husband is the most popular labor saving device ever invented.

∾

What's a man's idea of helping with the housework? Lifting his legs so you can vacuum around him.

∾

It is foolish to worry about something beyond your control — like your wife.

∾

She was married to an actor, then to a minister and last to an undertaker. One for the money, two for the show, three to get ready, and four to go."

∾

If love is blind, marriage is an eye-opener.

∾

Husband: "Honey, you have to admit, men have better judgment than women."
Wife: "I couldn't agree more. You married me and I married you."

∾

I lied on my income tax return. I listed myself as head of household.

∾

Weddings have become so costly that it is now the bride's father who breaks down and weeps.

∾

Doctor: "I don't like the way your husband looks."
Wife: "Neither do I, but he is good with the children."

∾

When he proposed, he vowed he'd go through hell for her. She's seeing to it that he does.

～

Alex decided not to get married because it's not honorable to sleep with a married woman.

～

Before they were married, he confessed that he was an atheist and did not believe there is a hell. Between his wife and mother-in-law, he is now convinced that he was wrong.

～

These days girls don't marry men to reform them. They want to get in on the fun.

～

She married a man for money. She divorced him for the same reason.

～

He: "Marriages are made in heaven."
She: "So are thunder and lightning."

～

What is a wooden wedding? That's when two Poles get married.

～

Marriage can be made in heaven, but we humans are responsible for the maintenance work.

～

Lulu's pretty frank. She says she ain't gonna sail on no sea of matrimony with no man until he's made a raft of money.

～

Ole and Lena got married. On their honeymoon trip, they were nearing the Twin Cities when Ole put his hand on Lena's knee. Lena said, "Ole, you can go farther if you want to." So Ole drove another 150 miles.

～

Ole had a heated argument with Mrs. Lindstrom. Finally, in exasperation, Mrs. Lindstrom exploded, "Ole, if you were my husband, I would give you poison. Not to be outdone, Ole retorted, "If you were my wife, I'd take it."

～

It was a friendly resort. The girls were all looking for husbands and the husbands were all looking for girls.

～

Clifford and Sophie have been married for twenty-five years and they still go out to dinner and dancing twice a week. She goes on Mondays and Wednesdays; he goes on Tuesdays and Thursdays.

∽

Lulu: "Do you love me?"
Roland: "Thirty-four years ago when we got married I told you I love you. If there is any change, I'll let you know."

∽

He could make some woman a lucky widow.

∽

Sue: "I never really knew the meaning of happiness until I got married."
Lulu: "I know exactly how you feel, but by that time, it's too late."

∽

Some husbands know all the answers because they've been listening all their lives.

∽

In Ireland, priests disapprove of sex before marriage because it holds up the marriage service.

∽

Marriage is nature's way of keeping people from fighting with strangers.

∽

Husband to wife: "Of course I like your relatives. I think your mother-in-law is a lot nicer than my mother-in-law."

∽

Husband: "Drinking makes you look beautiful."
Wife: "I haven't been drinking."
Husband: "But I have."

∽

Husband finding wife with lover: "What's going on here?"
Wife to lover: "See, I told you he was stupid."

∽

After he married an Amish girl, he drove her buggy.

∽

Sophie to Clifford after the wedding: "I'll stay out of your bill-fold if you'll stay out of my draw-ers."

~

Lulu was complaining to the minister because Alex did not talk to her for three days.
Minister: "How do you explain that, Alex?"
Alex: "I was waiting for her to stop talking. It isn't polite to interrupt."

~

Sven: "My wife plays golf with your wife."
Ole: "That's her problem."

~

Sign on a bridal store window: "We fit to tie."

~

Harry, getting ready to propose: "You look like my second wife."
Girl: "How many times have you been married?"
Harry: "Once."

~

The old-fashioned marriage called for the husband to be the head of the house — sort of a union leader.

~

Cain's wife divorced him because he wasn't Abel.

~

King Solomon had a thousand wives who did not have a headache.

~

The reason they don't give the groom a shower is because by now he is all washed up.

~

Every bride likes to be well-groomed.

~

She: "Who gave the bride away?"
He: "Not me. I kept my mouth shut."

~

Pastor: "When you married him, you married him for life."
Lulu: "Yes, but for the last five years, he hasn't shown any life."

~

Pastor: "Show your wife more affection."
Roland: "I did what you told me to do. I took her to a drive-in movie and let her look into the car windows."

~

Harry went to the courthouse to check when his marriage license expires.

~

The fellow who thinks marriage is a 50-50 proposition doesn't know much about fractions, women or marriage.

~

Maggie: "Why did I have to marry you to find out how stupid you are?"
Gus: "You should have known that when I asked you to marry me."

~

Roland threw away his wife's girdles. Now she's suing him for non-support.

~

Twenty years ago he said "I do," but he never did.

~

A girl who is fishing for a husband could end up with a worm.

~

Boss: "I know you can't get married on what I pay you. Some day, you'll thank me."

~

All a bachelor has to do to discover his hidden faults is to get married.

~

Sophie: "My husband once showered me with gifts, but lately, there's been a dry spell.

~

A good husband meets a marital crisis with a firm hand — full of flowers and candy.

~

The old-fashioned girl who darned her husband's socks now has a daughter who socks her darned husband.

~

The wife who dresses to please her husband wears last year's clothes.

~

It takes a smart husband to have the last word and not use it.

~

There is nothing like a dishtowel for wiping that contented look off a husband's face.

~

Sophie: "Did your husband have life insurance?"
Lulu: "No, he was a total loss."

~

When a woman laughs at her husband's jokes, either they're good jokes or she's a good wife.

~

The husband who brags that he never made a mistake has a wife who did.

~

When his wife nags, the civilized man goes to the club instead of reaching for one.

~

Marriages are made in heaven. That's why you have married couples harping at each other at bridge parties.

~

I asked an old friend, "Is your wife still as good looking?" He answered, "Yes, but it takes her an hour longer."

~

The divorce rate would be lower if people would marry for good instead of for better or for worse.

~

Judging from the specimens some girls select, you can't blame the bride for blushing.

~

George says: "It's much wiser to love thy neighbor than to love thy neighbor's wife."

~

Gus: "All marriages are happy. It's that living together afterwards that causes the problems."

~

Some men who speak with authority at work know enough to bow to a higher authority at home.

~

Some bachelors have no idea what married bliss is. Neither do some husbands.

~

Think before criticizing your wife's faults. Her defects may have prevented her from getting a better husband.

~

Alimony is a system in which one pays for the mistakes of two.

~

The ambition of some girls is to make a man a good husband.

~

Why are husbands and wives more courteous to strangers than to each other?

~

Judging by the divorce rate, many that said, "I do" didn't.

~

The old-fashioned girl is probably at home with her husband and children and probably remembers her first kiss, while some women can't remember their first husband.

~

Roland is well-informed. His wife just told him what she thinks of him.

~

The trouble with marriage is the personnel, not the institution.

~

No wonder so many marriages fail. Think of all the inexperienced people that get into them.

~

Clifford got seasick when he heard the words "embarking on the sea of matrimony."

~

The best music people can have in their home is domestic harmony.

~

Praise your wife. It may surprise her at first, but she'll appreciate your words. On the other hand, she may burst out crying thinking you're drunk.

~

Harry: "I'm thinking of getting married. What do you think of that?"
Maggie: "I think it's a great idea, if you ask me."

~

A young girl eloped wearing her father's trousers. The newspaper headline read: Flees in Papa's pants.

~

A man who had not kissed his wife in years shot and killed a man that did.

~

Some girls use a lot of soft soap to get a ring on their finger.

～

A thoughtful wife is one who has the pork chops ready when her husband comes home from a fishing trip.

～

I had sworn to be a bachelor. She had sworn to be a bride. But I guess you know the answer. She had nature on her side.

～

Visitor: "Where is that cute blond girl who was serving drinks a while ago?"
Hostess: "Why, I'll get you a drink if you're looking for one."
Visitor: "I'm not looking for a drink. I'm looking for my husband."

～

The trouble with a husband who works like a horse all day is that all he wants to do in the evenings is hit the hay.

～

One tried and true method of getting your wife home soon from out-of-town vacation is to send her a copy of the local paper with one item cut out.

～

Al: "Who was your mother before she was married?"
Sally: "I didn't have a mother before she was married."

～

A woman who was about to be married for the seventh time mailed invitations closing with the following remark: "Be sure to come. This is no amateur performance."

～

He: "If I had a million dollars, do you know where I'd be?"
She: "You'd be with me on our honeymoon."

～

Wife: "My husband is very possessive."
Counselor: "How so?"
Wife: "He refers to our wedding album as his owner's manual."

～

If that girl had grounds, she wouldn't divorce you. She would bury you.

～

Ex-wife: "He is six feet tall in his socks, and is five thousand dollars short in his alimony payments."

～

Women buy their husbands loafer shoes and leisure slacks, then call them lazy when they play the part they're dressed for.

∾

Some women have what it takes to wear the latest fashions — rich husbands.

∾

Husband to wife: "How do you expect me to remember your birthday when you never look any older?"

∾

If you think you have trouble supporting a wife, try not supporting her.

∾

Common sense could prevent many divorces; also many marriages.

∾

A husband called his wife overbearing because she had three sets of twins.

∾

No, you can't sue your marriage officiating minister for malpractice after or before the divorce.

∾

Nothing prepares a man for marriage as much as a girl.

∾

Whether a man winds up with a nest egg or a goose egg depends a lot on the kind of chick he marries.

∾

Clerk: "I'm sorry, but I can't issue a marriage license until you have a properly filled out form.
Girl: "Listen, buster, if my boyfriend doesn't care, why should you?"

∾

Little Sophie: "I hope to marry a rich man some day when my shape comes in."

∾

It doesn't seem right for a college to give a man with a wife and two children a bachelor's degree.

∾

My wife does bird imitations. She watches me like a hawk.

∾

Just because a woman is a fastidious housekeeper doesn't mean she should be constantly putting her husband in his place.

~

Fifty loggers and two women went into the woods. Later, one of the women married one of the loggers. Statistics show that two percent of loggers married fifty percent of the women.

~

A man who says he understands his wife probably lies about other things, too.

~

A wife's remarks can be very cutting, such as: "Go cut the grass," "Cut the hedge," etc.

~

Attorney: "You say your name is Miss Smith? I take it you are unmarried?"
Lulu: "Yes, twice."

~

Census taker: "What is your husband's average income?"
Wife: "About midnight."

~

A boy no sooner outgrows sticking out his tongue at girls than he sticks out his neck and gets married.

~

Wife: "You studied accounting in college, didn't you, dear?"
Husband: "Yes."
Wife: "Then account for that strange shade of lipstick on your shirt collar."

~

Doctor: "Good morning, Mrs. Smith. How's the pain in your neck?"
Dora: "He's fishing."

~

There's nothing like a marriage to break up a good romance.

~

A lady gave her husband a throw rug and told him to beat it. She hasn't seen him since.

~

Lester: "How is your wife?"
Roland: "Better than nothing."

~

Ella: "Are you keeping a hope chest?"
Lulu: "Heck, no. With a chest like mine, there is little hope."

~

Perhaps it is called "ground for divorce" because of the dirt.

～

In spite of all the talk about June brides, there are also some June grooms.

～

I read that a woman cremated her fourth husband. It doesn't seem right that some women don't have a husband and this woman had husbands to burn.

～

Max: "Who in your family made a brilliant marriage?"
Melvin: "My wife."

～

Causes for divorce are matrimony and alimony.

～

Jack: "Was your wife nervous the first time she asked you for money?"
Jim: "No, she was calm, and collected."

～

Lady: "I want to get a pistol for my husband."
Clerk: "Did he tell you what kind he wanted?"
Lady: "No, it's to be a surprise. He doesn't even know I intend to shoot him."

～

Roland: "Lulu, may I come along to the bridal shower? I'll bring the soap."

～

Many times when a man is in shape to buy his wife beautiful clothes, she is not.

～

It's hard for young wives to get used to being whistled for instead of at.

～

Pat: "Let me present my wife."
Mike: "No thanks, I have one of my own."

～

I read where a girl married a second lieutenant. The first lieutenant got away.

～

Lulu: "Every time I want to marry a man for love, I find out he has no money."

～

It's too bad that a girl can't get married without dragging some innocent young man to the altar with her.

Psychiatrists say that girls tend to marry men like their father. Now we know why mothers cry at their daughter's wedding.

Nowadays, some couples have their honeymoon first. If it's a success, they have their engagement, and if that works out well, they may have a wedding.

If you don't get along with your wife, don't get a divorce. It takes too long and is too costly. Buy her a nice bouquet of flowers. She will die from shock; then you can use the flowers at her funeral.

Wife to husband: "There is no electricity in the closet."
Husband: "Who do you think I am, Ben Franklin? Call an electrician."
Wife: "Will you replace these bulbs?"
Husband: "Who do you think I am, Thomas Edison? Call the repairman."
A few days later the wife said: "After you left this morning, the electrician came over here with his statement and told me I could pay him in cash, bake a cake or have sex."
Husband: "What kind of cake did you bake?"
Wife: "Who do you think I am, Betty Crocker?"

I was relaxing in my favorite chair reading the newspaper, watching a ballgame on TV and listening to another game on the radio, drinking beer, eating a snack and scratching the dog with my foot — and my wife had the nerve to accuse me of just sitting there doing nothing.

Reporter: "Sir, today you are mark-ing your 50th wedding anniversary and your 75th birthday. To what do you attribute your longevity, marital happiness and good health?"
Old man: "Well, Sonny, when we got married, my wife and I made a pact that when an argument came up, I was to go outdoors in order to give us both time to cool off. So I guess I have to attribute my longevity and good health to a vigorous outdoor life."

PERSONAL GROWTH
& VIRTUE

Learn from the mistakes of others. You can't live long enough to make all the mistakes yourself. I'm only seventy-nine years old and I've already learned something.

∼

The secret for happy living is not to do what you like but to like what you do.

∼

If you have push, you don't need pull.

∼

Don't be afraid to go out on a limb. That's where the fruit is.

∼

Cheerfulness is contagious. Don't wait to catch it from others. Be a carrier.

∼

Giving it another try is better than an alibi.

∼

Think what others ought to be like, then start being like that.

∼

If we can't do great things, we can do small things in a great way.

∼

Don't tell the world about your labor pains. Show them the baby.

∼

There is no man living who isn't capable of doing more than he thinks he can do.

∼

Often the difference between stumbling blocks and stepping stones is the way you use them.

∼

Don't be afraid of opposition. Remember, a kite rises against, not with, the wind.

∼

Poverty can best be overcome by confidence. Confidence comes from our accomplishments and having respect — both vital to eliminating poverty. Poverty can be internal as well as external.

∼

Nobody's perfect, but we could all use major renovation.

∼

You need to find both the key to success and the door to match the key.

~

It's good to put your best foot forward, just watch where you step.

~

If you take responsibility on your shoulders, there will be little room for chips.

~

The world owes you a living only when you have earned it.

~

A wise man learns much by the experience of others. An ordinary man learns by his own mistakes.

~

Knowledge is knowing a fact. Wisdom is knowing what to do with that fact.

~

Know when to speak your mind and when to mind your speech.

~

Just over the hill is a beautiful valley, but you must climb the hill to see it.

~

One way to break a bad habit is to drop it.

~

Human beings are actually happy only when they are striving for something worthwhile.

~

It is hard to recognize good luck. It looks so much like something you've learned.

~

You will never be better than when you are doing your best.

~

If you don't learn from your mistakes, there is no sense making them.

~

Defeat is not bitter unless you swallow it.

~

There is no greater waste than that of human talent.

~

Many waste so much time wishing for things they would already have if they hadn't spent so much time wishing.

~

A college doesn't give you knowledge, it just shows you where it is.

~

Those that complain most about the way the ball bounces are often the ones who dropped it.

~

If you let your yearnings get ahead of your earnings, you invite trouble.

~

Don't expect to stumble over anything good while sitting or lying down.

~

A wise man will make opportunities.

~

There is no harm in dreaming, as long as we get up and hustle when the alarm goes off.

~

Searching for happiness? It is usually close to home.

~

Life is tragic for those who have plenty to live on and have nothing to live for.

~

Success isn't how far you got but the distance you traveled from where you started.

~

If you want to excel, you often must step out of your comfort zone. Actions are controllable; emotions are not. Some procrastinators actually believe they are doing something. Be mindful of your goals.

~

When you can see crisis as an opportunity, your life doesn't become easier but more satisfying.

~

The symptoms of fatigue and laziness are almost identical.

~

Make the most of the best and the least of the worst.

~

Leaders are ordinary people who know where they are going and have extraordinary determination.

~

No one finds life worth living; one must make life worth living.

~

A strong leader doesn't worry about being on the right track. He makes the track.

~

Do what you can with what you have, right where you are.

~

There are no shortcuts to any place worth going.

~

The man who really wants to do something great will find a way; the other man will find an excuse.

~

Going down does not make you a failure, but staying down does. You must get up more often than you fall.

~

You are making progress if each mistake you make is a new one.

~

We cannot direct the winds, but we can adjust the sails.

~

Most of the things that come to the fellow who waits are not the things he was waiting for.

~

Learn to oppose peer pressure with a "no" that carries conviction.

~

We cannot become what we ought to be by remaining what we are.

~

When everything seems to be going against you, remember that an airplane takes off against the wind, not with it.

~

You'll never move up while running somebody down.

~

Following the line of least resistance is what makes both rivers and men crooked.

~

When you can think of yesterday without regret and tomorrow without fear, you are near real contentment, and well on the road to success.

~

You cannot have a better tomorrow if you are thinking about yesterday most of the time.

~

Greatness is not found in possessions, power, position or prestige. It is found in goodness, humility, service and character.

~

Greatness lies in the right use of strength.

~

Even failure is not entirely wasted. At least you know one more way something won't work.

~

Forget your mistakes. Just remember what they taught you.

~

I couldn't wait for success so I went ahead without it.

~

Our ends are joined by a common link. With one we sit, with one we think. Success depends on which we use. Heads we win; tails we lose.

~

A man becomes wise at his own expense.

~

The price of progress is change, and it takes all the change we have.

~

Digging for the facts is better mental exercise than jumping to conclusions.

~

A man can't make himself a place in the sun if he keeps taking refuge under the family tree.

~

The poorest of men is not the one without a cent; it's the man without a goal or dream.

~

Some people complain that the stepping stones to success bruise their feet.

~

If you don't get what you want, it's a sign that either you did not seriously want it or that you tried to bargain over the price.

~

To obtain a balanced personality, just forget your troubles as easily as you do your blessings.

~

Some folks spend all their time trying to get even when they ought to be trying to get ahead.

~

If you don't appreciate what you get, you should be thankful for what you have escaped.

~

Respect is earned, not commanded.

~

Advice is like medicine. You have to take it to find out if it does any good.

~

Blessed is the man who can laugh at himself. He'll never cease to amuse himself.

~

The surest way to gain respect is to earn it. True charity consists of helping those you have every reason to believe would not help you.

~

To be a leader, one must turn obstacles into stepping stones and disaster into triumph.

~

Too many people are eager to carry the piano stool when there is a piano to be moved.

~

Cultivate your virtues with confidence.

~

Character is not an inheritance. People must build it for themselves.

~

It is surprising to learn what heights one may attain merely by remaining on the level.

~

If you can smile at what you see in the mirror, there is hope for you.

~

Have character — don't be one.

~

It is easier to live up to a good name than to live down a bad reputation.

~

It isn't how high you go in life, but how you got there.

∼

Look for truth, inspire someone, lower your voice, make time for a young person, let your kindness come out, be happy. Happiness is not a destination. It is a way to travel.

∼

The real measure of our wealth is how much we would be worth if we lost all our money.

∼

A saver grows rich while seeming poor. A spender grows poor by seeming rich.

∼

When you stretch the truth, your story may look thin.

∼

Men of genius are admired; men of wealth are envied; men of power are feared; but only men of character are trusted.

∼

A mirror reveals to us both our best friend and our worst enemy.

∼

When you break your word, you break something that cannot be mended.

∼

It isn't what you have but what you are that makes life worthwhile.

∼

The true measure of a man's character is what he would do if he knew he would never be found out.

∼

Teaching children to count is not as important as teaching them what counts.

∼

We don't get dizzy from doing too many good turns.

∼

Courage is not the absence of fear, but the conquest of it.

∼

You must have principle to draw interest.

∼

Some people don't put their best foot forward until they get the other foot in hot water.

~

You may not be able to prevent people from forming a bad opinion of you, but you can keep them from being right.

~

Where we go and what we do advertises what we are.

~

A man has three names — the name he inherits, the name his parents gave him and the name he makes for himself.

~

If you want to test a man's true character, give him power.

~

Compromise is always wrong when it means sacrificing a principle.

~

There are two kinds of people who may never amount to much — those who cannot do what they are told and those who can do nothing else.

~

More people are flattered into virtue than bullied out of vice.

~

A good listener is not only popular, but after awhile he will know something.

~

A good example is like a bell that calls many to church.

~

In the race for quality, there is no finish line.

~

Nothing makes it easier to resist temptation than a proper upbringing, a sound set of values and witnesses.

~

The kind of ancestors we have is not as important as the kind of descendants our ancestors have.

~

Knowledge becomes wisdom only after it has been put to practical use.

~

Live your life in a manner that your autograph will be wanted instead of your fingerprints.

~

The time is always right to do what is right.

~

Many good intentions die young, but not because they were executed.

~

It is hard for the good to suspect evil. It is hard for the bad to suspect good.

~

The best tool that the devil has is a lie.

~

Be sincere with your compliments. Most people can tell the difference between sugar and saccharine.

~

Many rise to the occasion but few know when to sit down.

~

Reputation is one of the few things that looks worse when you try to decorate it.

~

Only you can damage your character.

~

Many children are taught virtues at mother's knee; vice at some other joint.

~

Most people don't need to be led into temptation. They usually find it on their own.

~

When a fellow tells you, "I'm going to tell you the truth," you wonder what he has been telling you up to now.

~

It is amazing how many folks will struggle to learn what is right and then not do it.

~

There is virtue even in fear. Without it, how long would we survive the hazards of daily life?

~

People who have to be led into temptation probably don't need to worry much.

~

Humble by nature and no reason to be otherwise.

~

How can some people with so little principle draw so much interest?

~

Some people are so busy being do-gooders, they don't have time to do any good.

~

Most of our faults are more pardonable than the methods we use to hide them.

~

The reason we recognize other people's faults so easily is because their faults are so much like our own.

~

Honesty is a question of right and wrong, not a matter of policy.

~

The key to everything is patience. You get chickens by hatching the egg — not by smashing it.

~

Following the path of least resistance is what makes rivers and men run crooked.

~

Modesty is very becoming to a man with great talent.

~

You may not be respected without being respectable.

~

Inflated pride could some day become hard to swallow.

~

A man without principle can't draw much interest.

~

One thing you can give and still keep is your word.

~

When a man won't listen to his conscience, it's usually because he doesn't want advice from a stranger.

~

A good example has twice the value of good advice.

~

The measure of a man's character is not what he gets from his ancestors but what he leaves his descendants.

~

Live so that no one will believe them when they speak ill of you.

~

Brains and beauty may be nature's gift. Character is your own achievement.

~

Wealth and poverty are two great tests of character.

~

Teaching children to count is not nearly as important as teaching them what counts.

~

Real style depends upon not what is on you but in you.

~

A little white lie can soil quickly.

GOVERNMENT
& POLITICS

A government big enough to give you everything you want is big enough to take everything you have.

~

In order to enjoy individual rights on a regular basis, we must carry a full dose of personal responsibility.

~

Freedom is the sure possession of those who have the courage to defend it.

~

With each privilege and right goes an equal amount of obligation and responsibility.

~

Every right and privilege implies a responsibility; every opportunity an obligation; every possession a duty.

~

It is better for an institution, a city, a state or a nation to be governed by good men and not merely by good laws.

~

Taxpayers are the casualties of the war on poverty.

~

Congressmen make the laws and their chaplains pray for our country.

~

We can be assured of peace when the caliber of the statesman is equal to the caliber of the guns. Peace won by compromise of principles is not an achievement.

~

Never in the history of America have so few loused up so much for so many.

~

It's easier to trim taxpayers than trim government expenses.

~

Taxation, like a lot of other things, is based on supply and demand. The government demands and we supply.

~

The United States of America has the highest standard of living in the world. Too bad we can't afford it.

~

You would think the ship of state would move quicker with all those bags of wind in Congress.

~

A politician is a person who follows public opinion and then calls himself a leader.

~

One should not talk about things one knows nothing about. People might think you're running for office.

~

The mess in Washington should not be blamed on one man. It took real teamwork.

~

The IRS sure knows how to gather money. You really have to hand it to them.

~

Modern politicians may be well versed in the questions of the day. They just don't know the answers.

~

The cheapest way to have your family tree traced is to run for office.

~

You hear that Congress spends money like drunken sailors. Actually, sailors spend their own money.

~

The concept of taxation is simple. You can shear a sheep repeatedly, but you can only skin it once.

~

Many politicians leave office because of illness and fatigue — people are sick and tired of them.

~

Maybe there should be an obedience school for politicians who renege on campaign promises.

~

Our candidate for president has never been a grafter. All he wants is a chance.

~

We wouldn't mind paying so much income tax if we knew which country was receiving our money.

~

Both the Russian constitution and the United States constitution guarantee freedom of speech. The big difference is the United States constitution guarantees freedom after speech.

~

If a politician had cannibals among his constituents, he would promise them missionaries for dinner.

∼

There is a vast difference between a horse race and a political race. In a horse race, the entire horse runs.

∼

Political jokes should not be elected.

∼

This country would not be going to the dogs if the elected officials had gone to obedience school.

∼

Most of the time we don't realize how much we have to be thankful for until April 15th when we have to pay taxes on it.

∼

In this generation, we have been subjected to so much media brainwashing that in the minds of people, government, not God, is our resource, and hope is in the welfare state.

∼

We all work for our government, but only the bureaucrats get paid for it.

∼

Too many people vote for whomever supports them in their best style. This movement is terminal and cannot continue much longer.

∼

Every dollar consumed by the government is a dollar not available to start a business or to generate jobs.

∼

In my will I requested that I be cremated and the ashes sent to the IRS with a note saying, "Now you have it all."

∼

I have never seen a donkey or an ass make a democrat out of himself.

∼

The largest line item in the federal budget is debt service.

∼

In the future, we must elect politicians that will sit and heel. We now have too many who merely roll over.

∼

Politics is the most promising of all careers.

∽

What we need are congressmen with more horse sense so we may obtain a stable government.

∽

If we must vote for a politician who is for the birds, make sure he or she is not another vulture.

∽

We do have complete control over how we pay our taxes - cash, check, credit cards or money orders.

∽

I was of the opinion that some of the political candidates were acting foolishly. Now I realize they were not acting.

∽

April 15th is the time of the year when we find that we owe much of our success to Uncle Sam.

∽

A lot of things being aired in Washington actually need fumigating.

∽

War may not decide which nation is right, but it can decide which nation is left.

∽

A southern farmer was introducing his family of boys to the president. "Seventeen boys," he said. "All are democrats except John, the little rascal. He got to readin'."

∽

The United States Senate opens with a prayer and closes with an investigation.

∽

The wages of sin should be subject to the income tax.

∽

My most expensive dependent is the United States government.

∽

Behind every successful man stands a woman and the IRS. One takes the credit, the other takes the cash.

∽

President Herbert Hoover gave his salary back to the government. Now the government wants everybody to do it.

∽

Why do politicians fight poverty with taxes?

~

Congress claims that our income tax is the fairest tax of all. It gives every individual an even chance at poverty.

~

An income tax return is like a girdle. If you put the wrong figure in it, you're apt to get pinched.

~

There are worse things than the income tax rate. Suppose we had to pay on what we think we are worth?

~

Our government is still trying to figure out ways to give things to people without first taking it away from others.

~

I can remember the day when a person that had to pay income tax was considered to be wealthy.

~

Some tax refunds are slower than a helicopter over a nudist camp.

~

If we don't change our ways, we need to change our national anthem to "Deep in the Heart of Taxes."

~

Progress: Our politicians have arranged to spend taxes before they collect them. They always talk "tax reform." We need some "spending reform."

~

Patrick Henry should see what taxation with representation is like.

~

Thousands of government workers are counting on you to stay on your job and pay your taxes.

~

The advantage of withholding taxes is that a fellow doesn't get so mad all at once.

~

The attitude of Congress toward hidden taxes is not to do away with them but to hide them better.

~

When we buy a leather billfold, we pay a luxury tax. The money we put into the billfold is taxed, followed by a sales tax when we remove the money.

~

The tax dollar goes many times farther today than it did sixty years ago. Today it goes all the way to the moon and beyond.

～

I can remember the good old days when Uncle Sam lived within his income and without most of ours.

～

Don't overtax yourself; the government will do it for you.

～

Ole and Sven decided to open a tailor shop in Washington D.C. They're sure to become rich because there are so many pressing problems there that need ironing out.

～

Washington has a large assortment of peace monuments. They build another one following every war.

～

Let's stop inflation. It's hazardous to our wealth.

～

I'm opposed to term limits. I think our congressmen should serve their full sentence.

～

The United Nations needs a firm law against any country waging war unless it fully pays for the war in advance.

～

The planks in his platform that looked so fine before the election started warping soon afterward.

～

When he first ran for office, he appealed to the voters, "I never stole anything in my life. All I ask is a chance."

～

For years he has paid his taxes with a smile. Now the Internal Revenue Service is after him for the cash.

～

Alex: "What do you think of these two candidates?"
Clifford: "I'm glad only one can be elected."

～

Electing two-bit politicians is no way to save our government big money.

～

When politicians get to the meat of the matter, it's usually baloney.

∼

The way Congress is spending money, it's no surprise that some of our banks bounced.

∼

Why are we surprised that Congress can't balance the budget? How much economic sense can we expect from people who spend millions of dollars to land a job that pays one hundred and fifty thousand dollars?

∼

The reason that politicians want to kick the crooks out of government is that they can't stand the competition.

∼

You can tell by the bark that he is political timber.

∼

What's needed in Washington is an immunization against staff infection.

∼

It might be better to pay our United Nations delegates a regular salary. Many don't seem to be very good at peace work.

∼

A number of years ago we hired a bunch of experts to get the donkeys out of the Grand Canyon. Could we obtain the same fellows to do the same good job in Washington?

∼

Judging from the taxes we pay, we don't have cheap politicians anymore.

∼

I'm glad we don't get as much government as we are paying for.

∼

A politician is a person who borrows your pot to cook your goose in.

∼

It's a sad state of affairs when Congress has to borrow a buck before they can pass it.

∼

Peace may cost as much as war, but it's a better buy.

∼

The confusion in Washington compares with the little boy who lost his gum in the chicken house.

∼

Everyone works for the government, either on the payroll or on the tax roll.

~

Giving help to the enemy used to be called treason. Now it's called foreign aid.

~

The only federally controlled enterprise that ever made money is the mint.

~

What we need is less government in business and more business in government. Old lady to the IRS clerk: "I do hope you will give my money to a nice country."

~

The first touch of spring is the IRS.

~

The IRS received a batch of buttons in the mail with this note: You got my shirt last year.

~

I would not mind giving our politicians all that free transportation if they would go where I want them to go.

~

What is hurting many Americans today is the high cost of low living.

~

The principle export of the United States is money.

~

In the United States we have complete separation of church and state. The church teaches that money isn't everything; the govern-ment tells us it is.

~

Isn't it remarkable how our pioneering ancestors built up a great nation without asking Congress for help?

~

A politician is a man who gets sworn in and then cussed out.

~

Politicians can do more funny things naturally than most of us can do purposely.

~

When politicians go to heaven, they play harps, because they're good at pulling strings.

≈

≈

A Minnesota politician announced that he fully understood the questions of the day. The trouble was that he didn't know the answers.

≈

All politicians will stand for what they think the voters will fall for.

≈

Money can't buy an honest politician.

≈

A politician was describing himself as the backbone of the legislature, but others said they wouldn't go quite that high.

≈

Give a politician a free hand and he will put it in your pocket.

≈

A political convention consists of a donkey, an elephant and a lot of bull.

≈

Most politicians are both liberal and conservative — conservative with their own money and liberal with ours.

Most politicians realize how difficult it would be to live under the laws that they helped pass. That's why they are so anxious to be reelected.

≈

A successful politician is one who can stay in the public eye without irritating it.

≈

Most folks were satisfied with their lot in life, until the politicians started to give them a free ride.

≈

They really are not cheap politicians. Take a good look at your tax bills.

≈

If you lie to people to get their money, that's fraud. If you lie to them to get their votes, that's politics.

≈

Why do we pay taxes we can't afford for services we don't use?

≈

Republicans think Santa Claus is a democrat — so do democrats.

≈

This candidate is using a picture showing him with his hands in his own pockets.

~

The purpose of any political campaign is to stay calm, cool and elected.

~

The radical left says it will work within the system. So do termites.

~

When a man runs for Congress, you are his friend. After he is elected, you are a constituent. When he's in office, you're just a taxpayer.

~

Clifford went into politics to make a name for himself. Now he gets called many names.

~

When reading what the republicans and democrats are saying about each other, it's no wonder that the Russians thought of us as being a warlike people.

~

Many would like to sue a congressman for breach of promise.

~

This country needs fewer rules and more good examples.

~

Today too many are fixing the blame and too few are fixing the trouble.

~

Can you hold congressmen responsible for anything they say while they are madly in love, drunk or running for office?

~

Businessmen create the prosperity that politicians take the credit for.

~

The door that shuts out freedom also shuts out protests.

~

Many politicians refuse to answer all your questions on the grounds that it might eliminate them.

~

Congress does some strange things. It puts a high tax on liquor, then raises the other taxes that drive people to drink.

～

The difference between communism and democracy is plenty.

～

The more government we have in the economy, the less economy we have in government.

～

Congress continues to appoint fact-finding committees, when what we really need are fact-facing committees.

～

We always feel relieved after paying our taxes — relieved of all we have.

～

After the first of the year, we'll see a lot of people sworn into office; and later on, there will be more swearing from unhappy constituents.

～

Conservatives try to solve economic problems; liberals subsidize them.

～

Inflation is nice to have in a tire but not in our country.

～

They elected Lulu chairman of the "Ways to be Mean Committee."

～

The Bureau of Internal Revenue is always looking for men who have what it takes.

～

Daylight savings is no way for Washington to produce better times.

～

To dress an American soldier, it takes the wool of two sheep and the hide of seven taxpayers.

～

Our government is not adding a surtax to be polite.

～

Some people wave the American flag but some waive what it stands for.

～

There is no costlier furniture than a government bureau.

～

What most countries ask of the United States is to be left a loan.

~

Fred: "Why would such a strong republican marry a democrat?"
John: "I think they wanted to start a third party."

~

Our country needs a cheaper way to make history.

~

Greta: "Where is the capitol of the United States?"
Hans: "In loans all over the world."

~

Dora says the Congressional Record must be one of those long-playing records.

~

I'm worried about Uncle Sam's rapidly expanding waste line. It's not healthy.

~

Our national budget needs less grafting and more pruning.

~

When Congress is in session, it's sort of like when a baby gets a hold of a hammer.

~

I'm going to vote a straight ticket as soon as I find out which party is totally straight.

~

We should all be proud to pay taxes in the United States. I could be just as proud paying half of the amount.

~

I fail to understand why a slight tax increase can cost you an extra thousand dollars and a substantial tax cut saves you only ninety-eight cents.

~

When Uncle Sam plays Santa, you wind up holding the bag.

~

Paying your income tax is for a good reason — such as keeping you out of jail.

~

A government bureau is where a taxpayer's shirt is kept.

~

On April 15th you count your blessings and send them to Washington.

~

We would like the federal government to follow our example and live within its means. The government should provide equality of opportunity but cannot and should not guarantee equal results.

∽

In 1913, Uncle Sam collected only thirteen million dollars in income taxes. That's why they're called the good old days. Inflation was something you did to a balloon and problems could be solved without raising taxes.

∽

Theodore Roosevelt once said, "The best leader is one who has sense enough to choose good men to do what he wants done and has the self-restraint to keep from meddling with them while they do it."

∽

There is a reliance on luck by many people, and they look upon the federal government as the source of that luck. Our goal should be to create our own luck. Most people have the qualifications to do just that.

∽

Our legislatures and courts have just about put sin out of business. They've made much of it legal. Then, we have some of the real old senators that are against everything they're too old to enjoy.

∽

If the American Indian would have had more stringent immigration laws, this country would not be in such a mess. Psalm to the welfare state: The government is my shepherd, therefore, I need not work. It allows me to lay down on the job. It leads me beside still factories, and it destroys all my initiatives. It leads into the path of a parasite for politics' sake. Yes, though I walk through the valley of laziness and deficit spending, I will fear no evil, for the government is with me. I prepare an economic utopia for me, by appropriating the earnings of my own grandchildren. It fills my head with false security, my insufficiency runs over. Surely the government should care for me all the days of life here on earth. And I shall dwell in a fool's paradise forever.

THOUGHTS
WHILE SHAVING

Disney CEO Michael Eisner sold his Disney stock for a $200 million profit. Now that's not bad for a Mickey Mouse operation.

≈

An elephant never forgets, but what does he have to remember?

≈

I read that somewhere in the world there is a woman having a baby every four seconds. Someone ought to find that woman and stop her.

≈

I read that the King of Siam had a herd of one hundred sacred elephants and over a thousand wives. That sure is a lot of elephants.

≈

A doctor calls the shots.

≈

Not only is hell hot — they have no deodorants.

≈

Pearl Harbor was bombed by Japan on December 7, 1941. I know a fellow who always gets bombed by midnight on December 31.

≈

The invention of the automobile has stopped a lot of horse stealing.

≈

Santa Claus is the only one who can run around with a bag all night and not get talked about.

≈

I don't think we will ever have a high-class restaurant in outer space. They just don't have the atmosphere.

≈

Overstuffed things at our house are not all furniture.

≈

No, the bald spot on the back of my head is not a solar panel for a heart pacer.

≈

The hardest thing about ice skating is the ice when you come right down to it.

≈

I think the reason that our pioneers went across the country in a covered wagon is because they didn't want to wait forty years for a train.

≈

It is better to be patient on the road than to be a patient in the hospital.

~

A careful driver is known by the fenders he keeps.

~

A cautious man is one who hasn't let a woman pin anything on him since he was a baby.

~

In the Old West, the judges would not sentence the bad guys; they would suspend them instead.

~

If you are not careful as you slide down the banister of life, you may get a splinter in your career.

~

Many a romance has started with a bottle of corn and ended up with a full crib.

~

Your car could be recalled by the maker if there is a defect in your bank account.

~

The only thing you can still do on a shoestring is trip.

~

The death penalty may not eliminate crime, but it will stop repeaters.

~

If medical science has made so much progress, why do I feel so much worse than I did forty years ago?

~

The universe is made up of protons, electrons, neutrons and morons.

~

The chaplains who pray for the United States Senate and House of Representatives actually should pray for the taxpayers.

~

A short-armed fisherman is not as big a liar as a long-armed fisherman.

~

It is good that people do change, otherwise, their clothes would smell unpleasant.

~

Today Robin Hood would have to steal from the poor because the rich carry only credit cards.

~

When you stop to think, don't forget to start again.

≈

In baseball, the bases get loaded; in football, the spectators get loaded.

≈

Twenty-dollar bills have become very fragile. It seems we break one every time we go into a grocery store.

≈

What's the big deal about liquid diets? Many people go on liquid diets. They're called drunks.

≈

If I work real hard and save my money, some day I'll have enough wealth to share it with those who don't work and save.

≈

I do believe carrots are good for your eyes. I have never seen a rabbit with glasses.

≈

All people have weaknesses. Some have mighty strong weaknesses.

≈

Little boys who don't always tell the truth will probably grow up to become weather forecasters.

≈

Refresh yourself. Put your tongue on a very cold pump handle.

≈

Many a Hollywood actress won't wear a dress that's not original, but they'll take a secondhand husband.

≈

If it were as easy to borrow money from the bank as the advertisements claim, why would anybody want to rob a bank?

≈

Advice is what you get when you are not going to get anything else.

≈

Some people are willing to serve in an advisory capacity only.

≈

Even a clock that's not running tells the correct time twice a day.

≈

There are two finishes for automobiles: lacquer and liquor.

~

An automobile should not have more horsepower in its engine than horse sense in the driver.

~

After buying a used car, I soon found out how hard it is to drive a bargain.

~

It seems foolish to spend so much time loving your enemies when we should be treating our friends a little better.

~

Wouldn't it be wonderful if everybody behaved as he thinks the other person ought to behave?

~

In this day and age, you can't really afford to be poor.

~

There are so many legal ways to be dishonest. Why take up crime?

~

A dentist is the only man on earth who can tell a woman when to open or close her mouth and get away with it.

~

Some people with credit cards buy things they don't need, to impress people they don't like, with money they don't have.

~

I should stop weight lifting with a knife and fork.

~

I can't reduce my weight by talking about it. I must keep my mouth shut.

~

If it weren't for the divorce courts separating people, the police would have to do it.

~

Some people who make the most bread can be the biggest crumbs.

~

The only thing that is still dirt cheap is dirt.

~

If I get to the point of having money to burn, I'm sure there will be some opportunist to offer me a match.

~

People who complain about the high cost of living should check out funeral prices these days.

∼

Whoever said "better late than never" obviously was never audited.

∼

There are many things in life more important than money, but it takes money to buy them.

∼

It isn't wise to tell our children the value of money. This will discourage them.

∼

Despite the cost of living today, living is still popular.

∼

The way some people hold on to money, you'd think it was worth the paper it was printed on.

∼

I read about two fellows who stopped writing when they became pen pals. They were committed to the same prison for passing bad checks.

∼

After paying all your bills each month, about the only thing left to spend is a nice quiet evening at home.

∼

The meek may inherit the earth, but it will be the others who'll hold the mortgages.

∼

A dreamboat has been known to sail right through someone else's liquid assets.

∼

Will power could make your heirs very unhappy. Have you made a will?

∼

Spend each day as if it were your last, and you'll be broke in six months.

∼

The rush hour traffic would not be so bad if you could avoid the lush hour part.

∼

Considering all the things that now have to be taken with a grain of salt, we'll have a salt shortage soon.

∼

In some neighborhoods, instead of asking what time it is, they take your watch.

≈

When the chips are down, you might as well get the dip out, too.

≈

Whenever somebody gives me a snow job, I'm the one left to shovel it.

≈

Porcupines do have their points.

≈

Some folks think that the way to rise above the crowd is to be full of hot air.

≈

So Humpty Dumpty had a great fall. How was the rest of his year?

≈

A thought about chicken noodle soup: if the chicken had used his noodle, he wouldn't be in the soup.

≈

If you really want to lead a stable life, move into a barn.

≈

There is more than one way to skin a cat, but who wants to know?

≈

The best way to have pen pals without ever writing a letter is to be a pig.

≈

Blunt people always come to the point.

≈

It's not so easy to get a parking ticket. First you have to find a parking place.

≈

Lots of people have the gift of gab; few know how to wrap it up.

≈

In this country, you are innocent until proven guilty — or until you publish your memoirs.

≈

You can obtain pierced ears by merely listening to hard rock music.

≈

How can soap operas be so dirty?

≈

Do you think anyone ever told Ben Franklin to "go fly a kite?"

～

Did you hear about the student who took a crash course in flying?

～

A sure way to be good at golf is to be bad at arithmetic.

～

Kids need to eat their vegetables so they'll grow up strong enough to make their kids eat their vegetables.

～

The FBI has over a hundred million fingerprints. So does every home with three or more kids.

～

The best time to change someone is when they are a baby.

～

We want our kids to have all the things we didn't have as children — like good grades.

～

Horses have horse sense. That's why they don't bet on people.

～

Don't take it too seriously when a pretty girl smiles at you. She may just be getting ready to laugh out loud.

～

A lot of guys who look like princes end up being toads.

～

You know you're in a small town when people don't use their turn signal because everybody knows where they're going.

～

You know you're in a small town when you miss a Sunday at church and your pastor mails you a get well card.

～

Love thy neighbor, or else you'll never get back the power tools you loaned him.

～

Psychiatrists tell us that one out of every four Americans is mentally ill. If I check out three of my friends and they seem all right, does that mean me?

～

Many families go in for water sports — like dishwashing and baby bathing.

∼

Statistics show that two out of three families live next door.

∼

Success is relative. The more success, the more relatives.

∼

With the price you pay for a private hospital room, you would expect better than a semi-private gown.

∼

New York wants to get rid of its pigeons and Las Vegas wants to get more pigeons.

∼

Alcoholics should not drive while drinking. They might spill their liquor.

∼

Has anyone ever injured their eyes by looking on the bright side of things?

∼

Headline: Two convicts evade noose; jury hung.

∼

Transplanting body parts is not new. The first was a rib from Adam to Eve.

∼

I read that laughter makes the world go 'round. I think it's because there are so many clowns running the world.

∼

A genuine sense of humor is the pole that adds balance to our steps as we walk the tightrope of life.

∼

Don't depend on a rabbit's foot. It didn't work for the rabbit.

∼

A slot machine is something like a voting machine. You pull down a lever and more often than not, you get nothing.

∼

I read that Norvel was fighting for Lulu's honor, which is more than she ever did.

∼

The reason many people get lost in thought is that it's such unfamiliar territory.

∼

It is not difficult to make a mountain out of a molehill. Just add dirt.

∼

I heard that your son goes to college on a scholarship. That's better than walking.

∼

The reason so many kids have an identity problem these days is because many parents ask, "Just who do you think you are?"

∼

I've been estimating the weight of chickens for seventy years and have always come within five pounds.

∼

They raise a lot of hops in the Vancouver, Canada area. Hops are used for brewing beer. Rabbits also use a lot of hops.

∼

Even Adam and Eve had to turn over a new leaf.

∼

A good time to keep your mouth shut is when you are in deep water.

∼

If you get out of life only what you put into it, how do you keep up with inflation?

∼

A self-made man should not worship his creator.

∼

Vaudeville died. Television is the box they buried it in.

∼

Some people cause happiness whenever they come. Others cause happiness whenever they go.

∼

I think I can survive everything except death.

∼

She was only a horseman's daughter, but all the other horsemen knew her.

∼

Experts report that our drinking water is bad because of the chemicals in it, but not as bad as it would be if the chemicals were left out.

∼

Will our children follow our example or our advice?

~

When you realize how much you don't know, are you beginning to get smart?

~

If it were not for the doers, the critics would be out of business.

~

The guy whose troubles are behind him is a school bus driver.

~

Applied child psychology was more effective when the proper applicator was used.

~

Mosquitoes put more clothes on people than does modesty.

~

Some girls show a lot of style, and some styles show a lot of girl.

~

You are never fully dressed until you wear a smile.

~

It's unfortunate that common sense is not more common.

~

Horse sense is what keeps a woman from being a nag.

~

The trouble with all these square meals is they have made me so round.

~

I like people, however, there are some I would like to change a little.

~

The Minnesota Twins are going to have poor attendance this year. They lost some of their pitchers. They also lost their opener, so the beer drinkers will stay home.

~

It's no use to complain about winter. Winter comes in one year and out the other.

~

Our neighbor lady would not allow her daughter to go out with an inventory clerk.

~

A fortuneteller must enjoy her work. She always has a ball.

~

After all is said and done, more is said than done.

~

If the world is getting smaller, why do they continue to raise the price of postage stamps?

~

All that many youngsters want to get out of school is themselves.

~

A cow can convert grass into milk. I'm sure that many of our scientists wish they could do that.

~

It's hard to raise a family, especially in the morning.

~

The dictionary must be wrong. It says the dumb can't talk.

~

Most of us make enough money to pay our taxes. What we need is something to live on after that.

~

Some TV anchormen/women receive eight times as much money to read the news as the president of the United States gets to make the news.

~

We are told that television is still in its infancy. Is that why we have to change the channel so often?

~

Children who watch television every evening will go down in history, not to mention reading, spelling, math, geography and science.

~

There is always something to be thankful for. If you can't pay your bills, you can be thankful you're not one of your creditors.

~

A committee often keeps minutes and wastes hours.

~

People scratch themselves because they are the only ones who know where they itch.

~

Boomerangs are making a comeback.

~

Pleasant memories must be arranged for in advance.

~

Watch the man who says he is the boss at home. He may lie about other matters, too.

~

Oxygen was discovered 185 years ago. I wonder what the poor people did before that?

~

My doctor gave me some pills to build up my body. I don't have enough strength to get the cap off the bottle.

~

Babies are subject to change without notice.

~

An English bulldog looks like he has been chasing parked cars.

~

Let's quit trying to understand women. Just enjoy having them around.

~

If you didn't make mistakes, you might live and die without ever hearing your name mentioned.

~

When you are in the examining room waiting for your doctor, why does he knock before he comes in?

~

I asked a young lady about her cold. She gave me a blow-by-blow account.

~

Health insurance is like wearing a hospital gown. You only think you are covered.

~

Jack said he was the most important man on the council. He merely made that statement because he thought he was under oath.

~

Was Samson the first showman when he brought the house down?

~

Edison invented the phonograph. Later, he invented the light bulb so people could see where to place the needle on the records.

~

The birds and bees were trailing Sam and taking notes.

~

Some men are always doing the town, but not doing the town much good.

~

I don't think it is the minutes spent eating that puts all that weight on you. It's the seconds.

~

Some speakers are good, some speakers are boring, and some are good and boring.

~

Whenever a person gets something without earning it, some other person has to earn something without getting it.

~

If George Washington were alive today, he would be an old man.

~

Only lawyers can write a five-thousand-word document and call it a brief.

~

Many a woman has started out playing with fire and ended up cooking over it.

~

A racehorse is an animal that can take hundreds of people for a ride at the same time.

~

The best way to hear money jingle in your pockets is to shake a leg.

~

A dirty old man is a father of four daughters with only one bathroom.

~

You can never tell about a woman. Besides, you shouldn't.

~

The world is not interested in the storms you encountered but if you brought in the ship.

~

One learns manners from those who have none.

~

Spilled on the earth are all the joys of heaven.

~

I read that everyone should spend some time on self-analysis. I don't know much about this self-analysis business. Urinalysis I know.

～

Farmer Olson's hens stopped laying eggs. They got sick of working for chicken feed.

～

Arnold the chicken farmer had an alarm cluck.

～

What about the egg that chickened out?

～

Confucius say: "Duck who fly up-side down will quack up."

～

An orthopedic surgeon gets all the breaks.

～

Gus didn't have the Vegas idea of how to get to Nevada.

～

You have to make allowances for kids — payable weekly.

～

You should always forgive your enemies. Nothing annoys them more.

～

You have grown up on the day you have the first good laugh at yourself.

～

I'm so glad to be back home that I'm glad I went.

～

Seventy-eight percent of the earth is covered with water and the other twenty-two percent is covered with mortgages.

～

Our big mistake is to love things and use people.

～

The value of a dollar will never drop as low as some people will stoop to get it.

～

My hunting is confined to shooting pool, craps and bull.

～

Dough is the wrong term for money. Dough sticks to your hands.

∼

When someone says, "Have a nice day," tell them you have other plans, then watch their reaction.

∼

Aerobic workouts are nothing new. Back on the farm, they called them chores.

∼

Americans must be religious people. Judging by the way that they drive, you can tell that they trust in God.

∼

Even the best running cars have some jerks in them.

∼

We can't expect much prison reform until we send a better class of people to prison.

∼

While we are ridding our country of communism, socialism and fascism, let's include rheumatism.

∼

On my first day out as an insurance salesman, I received two orders — "get out" and "stay out."

∼

Most folks were satisfied with their lot in life, until the politicians started giving them free rides.

∼

I could have had any girl I pleased, but I didn't please many of them.

∼

Don't advertise your troubles. There's no market for them.

∼

It is not the ship in the water but the water in the ship that sinks it.

∼

Men are here to stay. Let's make the best of them.

∼

A teacher who comes to class real early is in a class all by herself.

∼

The next time you go in an antique store, ask "What's new?"

∼

A lawn mower gets very poor gas mileage — only one yard to a gallon.

∼

Do we have enough crutches in the world for all the lame excuses?

~

Not all people leave a vacancy when they leave.

~

I've heard that the only reason some people can keep their heads above water is that wood floats.

~

These are the good old days I'm going to miss many years from now.

~

Man does not live by bread alone. He needs buttering up occasionally.

~

Some baloney is disguised as food for thought.

~

Some tasks have to be put off dozens of times before they will completely slip your mind.

~

Many people have their home on the outskirts of their income.

~

If your wife wants to learn to drive, don't stand in her way.

~

A girl can be scared to death by a mouse or a spider, but she's often too willing to take her chances with a wolf.

~

Women and men agree on one issue — they distrust women more than men.

~

Many old-timers spend their time living in the past. Some of my past was not that pleasant.

~

My doctor told me that I can't play golf. He's not the first one to tell me that.

~

Most people have nice things said about them at their funeral. They miss hearing them said by only a few days.

~

Most of the measurable warming of our planet occurred before 1950. The heavy energy consumption came after 1950.

I heard of a fellow in North Dakota who gave up drinking, smoking, rich food and women. He was healthy right up to the day he committed suicide.

Free enterprise has not been the destroyer of inner cities.

Many scientists don't believe that freon gas used in refrigeration ever caused or contributed to holes in the ozone. Why spend two to three trillion dollars to convert to a substitute?

Today many Americans look at lawsuits the way they look at lotteries. Is this the American way as we knew it fifty years ago? The practice is as unjust as the "deep pockets rule" in our justice system.

Of all the things that fly, time is the fastest.

The presents that come wrapped in love are the best presents you can ever receive, no matter how inexpensive.

Be thankful for all the good things that we have; also be thankful for all the bad things that we don't have.

In an atomic war, all men will be cremated equal.

When a wife is up in the air and harping about something, that doesn't necessarily make her an angel.

The average man wants a roof over his head and likes to raise it occasionally.

Twenty years from now, all of today's beautiful women will be fifteen years older.

A leader who keeps his ear to the ground may expose his rear end.

Our taste sure changes as we mature. Little girls like painted dolls and little boys like soldiers. When they grow up, the girls like the soldiers and the boys like the painted dolls.

~

People should not trace their family tree too far because they may find the tree that their family lived in.

~

Don't be too hard on your relatives. They had no choice in the matter either.

~

When you play golf, nothing counts like your opponent.

~

Some people drive their automobiles as though they were rehearsing for an accident.

~

If God had wanted us to use the metric system, there would have been twenty disciples.

~

When I went into business, I didn't have much money, but I had two bankers who did.

~

I still don't have much money in blue chip stocks. My chips are more like the buffalo chip variety.

~

It's not the ups and downs of life that bother the average person. It's the jerks.

~

Most of us would have more trouble than we have if all our prayers had been answered.

~

A good way to stay young is to live honestly, eat sensibly, sleep well, work hard, worship regularly, and lie about your age.

~

Stealing a kiss may be petty larceny but sometimes it's grand.

~

In the language of flowers, the yellow rose means friendship, the red rose means love, the orchid means business.

~

If we don't solve the energy crisis, the sheik will inherit the earth.

~

I understand that France wants to buy the Rock of Gibraltar from Spain and name it DeGaulle Stone.

If you live within your income, you'll live without worry — and without a lot of other things.

～

I can't get the English Channel on my TV set.

～

One half of being smart is to know what you are dumb at.

～

Luck is a matter of preparation meeting opportunity.

～

God gave us five senses — touch, smell, sight, hearing and taste. The successful person has two more — horse and common.

～

You can't do much about the length of your life, but you sure can do a lot about its depth and width.

～

When it comes to electing a United States president, we only have two choices; when we elect a Miss America we have a choice of fifty.

～

Worry is like a rocking chair. It gives you something to do, but it doesn't get you anywhere.

～

Medical science is adding years to our lives. Adding life to our years is our job.

～

A young fellow tried to use a letter from Ed McMahon as collateral to buy a $400,000 home.

～

Did you know: That Isaac Newton did poorly in grade school? That Caruso's music teacher told him he couldn't sing and that he had no voice at all? That Admiral Richard Byre had been retired from the Navy as "unfit for service" until he flew over both Poles? That an editor told Louisa May Alcott she could never write anything that had popular appeal?

～

I believe there are only two groups of things you should worry about: the kind you can control — these need corrective measures at once, even if you must get out of bed at three a.m. to attend to matters. (In that event, you can't sleep anyhow.) The kind of worry you can't do anything about should not absorb your energy or bring loss of sleep. That leaves only one valid worry that requires attention.

～

Under the Constitution of the United States, every man has the right to make a fool of himself as he sees fit. Our freedom also includes the right to mismanage our own affairs. Americans have always been willing to pay any price for freedom. If you don't believe it, look at the divorce statistics. Some people forget that freedom is a package deal — with it comes responsibilities and consequences. Freedom is not the right to do as you please, but the liberty to do as you ought. I hope we'll continue to have the courage to defend our freedom.

～

The queen of England has announced she will soon begin paying taxes on her income, just like everybody else. Although she may be entitled to the same deductions as everybody else, I think she's way out of line trying to write off the thirteen colonies as a business loss.

～

TOASTS

▲ My parting advice is to put a little water on your comb.

▲ Drive carefully. Don't insist on your rites.

▲ For that run-down feeling, try jaywalking.

▲ As you slide down the banister of life, may the splinters never point your way.

▲ Wishing all my friends a long life and may they be in heaven sixty minutes before the devil knows they're dead.

▲ May God and your luggage be with you always.

~

Pennsylvania Dutch Dialect:
- ▲ Let's walk the street down.
- ▲ Throw the horse over the fence some hay.
- ▲ The hurrier I go, the behinder I get.
- ▲ Throw papa down the stairs his hat.

WORK

The key to success is setting aside eight hours per day for work and eight hours per day for sleep, then making sure they are not the same set of hours.

~

We'll always have business cycles. That's why we all must pedal.

~

Your mistakes may be proof that at least you tried to accomplish something.

~

The best time to do something is between yesterday and tomorrow.

~

The right angle to approach a difficult problem is the "try-angle."

~

Never mind the business outlook. Be on the lookout for business.

~

Many people quit looking for work after they have found a job.

~

Increase your net profit. Sell more nets.

~

If there is anything small, shallow or ugly about a person, giving him a lot of authority will bring it out.

~

We have too many people who prefer to vote for something they want rather than work for it.

~

A man is not rewarded for having brains but for using them.

~

If you itch for something, you must scratch for it.

~

No life grows great until it is focused, dedicated and disciplined.

~

You can't help men permanently by doing for them what they could and should do for themselves.

~

Don't worry about things you can't control. Keep yourself busy controlling the things that depend on you.

~

Hard work is the key to success. Some people would rather pick the lock.

∼

People who do most of the knocking don't seem to know how to ring the bell.

∼

Ideas won't work unless you do.

∼

Could our dollar do as much for us as it once did? Are we willing to do as much as we once did for a dollar?

∼

Take the road to creativity and get off your dead end.

∼

The only thing that ever sat its way to success was a hen.

∼

A person who fiddles around seldom gets to lead the orchestra.

∼

The person who is busy pulling on the oars doesn't have time to rock the boat.

∼

Talent is what you are blessed with. Skill is how you take care of that gift.

∼

A fellow can learn more by listening. Anything he can say, he already knows.

∼

You don't need good connections to become an electrician. Make your own.

∼

You can't climb to the top of the ladder without getting a few splinters.

∼

Most people don't mind going to work. It's the work they don't like.

∼

One reason experience is such a good teacher is it doesn't allow any dropouts.

∼

The fact that the world was created in six days shows what could be done before coffee breaks, wage and hour laws, etc.

∼

People who are really on the ball are usually at the bottom of a pile of football players.

～

Most people who are aimless don't have the ammunition anyway.

～

With all the yield signs along the way, the road to success isn't easy, but success can be obtained without a textbook.

～

Many people miss their calling because they can't hear their call over the noise they make while looking for a free lunch. Others wait to have a free lunch delivered.

～

Some people carve their way to success and others just chisel it.

～

How do people expect to get ahead when they spend money seven days a week and only work five?

～

Many an optimist has become rich by buying out a pessimist.

～

People learn the value of money while working for it or by trying to borrow it.

～

The failure is in the person who holds the job, not in the job.

～

There are splinters in the ladder of success, but you don't notice them until you slide down.

～

You can't climb the ladder of success if you stand around waiting for the elevator.

～

If you cannot win, make the one ahead of you break the record.

～

How many days does it take you to do a day's work?

～

The reason many people can't find opportunity is because it is often disguised as hard work.

～

Successful people do a little more than they are required to do.

~

It's simply fantastic the amount of work you can do if you don't do anything else.

~

Work is hard when there is something else you would rather do.

~

If at first you don't succeed, try the outfield.

~

When starting a new business from scratch, you first get the scratch. That's the hard part. After you have the scratch, the bank will lend you money.

~

Ability will enable a man to get to the top, but it takes character to keep him there.

~

Some fellows dream of worthy accomplishments while others stay awake and do them.

~

People might doubt what you say, but they will believe what you actually do.

~

A man with a burning ambition is seldom fired.

~

You can make your business good by yearning, learning and earning.

~

If you wish to become an achiever, you must first become a believer.

~

If everyone were perfectly contented, there would be no progress.

~

It's no help to put your best foot forward if you drag the other.

~

A fellow who waits to be told won't be told to do big things.

~

It is much better to pick the fruit than to wait for it to fall.

~

Big potatoes are on top of the heap because there are a lot of little potatoes holding them up.

~

Cranks do not turn the wheels of industry.

～

You can't expect time to work for you if you keep killing it.

～

The biggest mistake you can make is to believe that you are working for someone else.

～

The man who rolls up his sleeves seldom loses his shirt.

～

You can't plow a field by turning it over in your mind.

～

We should all be sincerely concerned about earning it instead of making it.

～

If money is all you want, money is all you get.

～

It is not enough to be able to see through things; you must be able to see things through.

～

Optimism is a necessary ingredient for success.

～

The road to success runs uphill, so don't expect to break any speed records.

～

If we sit down and wait for success, failure will catch up with us.

～

People become well to do by doing what they do well.

～

You can carve out a future if you don't whittle away your time.

～

It's generally the fellows who have not planted anything who sit around waiting for their harvest.

～

Solve problems, don't be one of them.

～

When your work speaks for itself, don't interrupt.

~

Work can be fun. The only real reward that life offers is the thrill of achievement.

~

Be convinced of the necessity of saving one half a year's salary before indulging in any luxury.

~

Remember this on your way up. The biggest dog was once a pup. This is true, no ifs or buts, the tallest trees once were nuts.

~

Effort counts. A room may be dark because the sun is not shining, or it may be dark because the windows are dirty. You can't turn on the sun, but you can wash the windows.

~

Don't be discouraged by the job you can't do — just do the job you can do. You will be surprised how effective that will be.

~

We'll have good times when everybody who has a job is working.

~

Ambition can get you into a lot of hard work, but doing nothing could be very tiresome because you can't stop and rest.

~

No business opportunity is ever lost. If you fumble it, your competitor will find it.

~

Many people should be happy for not being paid what they are worth.

Automation has opened up a whole new field of unemployment.

~

The only way some people can be paid what they are worth is if the minimum wage law is abolished.

~

The one who is watching the clock during a coffee break is the boss.

~

The world is full of willing people. Some are willing to work and some are willing to let them.

~

When something difficult becomes easy, you've become a professional in that area.

~

To get up in the world, you must get up in the morning.

~

Men who complain that their boss is dumb would be out of a job if he were any smarter.

~

Boss: "For this job, we want someone who is very responsible."
Employee: "That's me. Everywhere I've ever worked, whenever something went wrong, I was responsible."

~

At a luncheon meeting, the man next to the banker said, "Someone told me you're looking for a cashier."
Banker: "Yes, that's right."
Man: "But didn't you just hire one last month?"
Banker: "Precisely, that's the one we're looking for."

~

Andy: "Boss, I came to see if you could raise my salary."
Boss: "Don't worry. I've managed to raise it every month so far, haven't I?"

~

Boss: "I'm planning a salary increase for you, young man."
Roland: "When does it become effective?"
Boss: "Just as soon as you do."

~

By faithfully working eight hours a day, you may eventually get to be a boss and then work sixteen hours a day.

~

Boss: "You should have been here at eight this morning."
Secretary: "Why? What happened?"

~

Salesman to customer: "This is actually a fire sale. The boss said that if I don't make a sale, I'm fired.

~

Enthusiasm for hard work is most sincerely expressed by the person who is paying for it.

~

A great deal of poor health in this country may be attributed to heavy meals and light work.

~

Make hay with the grass that grows under other people's feet.

~

A salesman need never be ashamed of his calling. He should only be ashamed of his not calling.

~

Many traveling salesmen are men who wish they had as much fun on the road as their wives think they have.

~

Old salesmen never die; they merely get out of commission.

~

If you want your dreams to come true, don't oversleep.

~

It's not the number of people employed in a business that makes it successful. It's the number of people working.

~

If the key to success doesn't fit your ignition, try more aspiration and perspiration.

~

An American can consider himself a success when it costs him more to support the government than to support a wife and children.

~

Even a woodpecker has discovered that the only way to succeed is to use one's head.

~

Work keeps a lot of people from being a success.

~

No man wakes up to find himself successful.

~

There are many keys to success, but the locks seem to be changing.

~

It may take years to become an overnight success.

~

No one has ever traveled the road to success on a pass, but on the ability to do better than good enough.

~

Behind every successful man there is a woman competing for the job.

~

My take-home pay could hardly survive the trip, and then it wouldn't stay home.

~

You cannot lift the wage earner by pulling down the wage payer. Wages can't meet higher consumer prices if they're both going in the same direction.

~

What's all this talk about getting rich the hard way? Is there any other way?

~

Sign in supermarket: Wanted — Clerk to work eight hours to replace one who didn't.

~

Two things deprive people of their peace of mind — work unfinished and work not begun.

~

About the only way work can kill a fellow is to scare him to death.

~

Work hard. The job you save may be your own.

~

Not only should you be a jump ahead of the other fellow, you must be headed in the right direction.

~

Years ago, when you saw a bunch of fellows on the street with shovels, etc., you knew what they were doing. These days they're erecting a sign "Men Working."

~

Opportunity is frequently over-looked because it disguises itself as work.

~

No job is too difficult for someone with vision and the power to delegate.

~

Ability without ambition is like a car without a motor.

~

He worked hard to get to the top of the ladder, only to find that he'd leaned it against the wrong wall.

~

When opportunity knocks, don't complain about the noise.

~

You can tell he isn't afraid of work. Look at the way he fights it.

≈

Our meeting went like clockwork. We went around in circles all day.

≈

It's easy to separate winners from losers. Winners know when opportunity knocks; losers knock every opportunity.

≈

The owner of a company offered a two hundred dollar prize for the best money-saving idea. First prize went to the employee who suggested the amount be cut to one hundred.

≈

Some people think that opportunity is a chance to get money without working for it.

≈

If you really want to get ahead in your work, become a hairdresser.

≈

You can always tell luck from ability by its duration.

≈

In a union shop a worker can get into trouble for resisting a rest.

≈

I know a business executive who gave his employees long vacations to find out which ones he could do without.

≈

What worries me is the large number of unemployed still on the payrolls.

≈

Imagine yourself without a job. Now, do you appreciate your job? If that's not enough, read all the ads and discover all the jobs you're not equipped to handle.

≈

Many people today want to get to the Promised Land without going through the wilderness. Like farmers, we need to learn that we can't sow and reap the same day.

≈

Many Americans think it's easier to vote for what they want than to work for it.

≈

Boss: "I wish you wouldn't whistle when you work."
Roland: "I wasn't working, sir."

~

When a friend of mine retired, instead of giving him a gold watch, they just told him the time. That's really scaling back.

~

There's no real substitute for brains, but silence does pretty well.

~

Executive ability is the art of getting credit for all the hard work that someone else does.

~

Staying in business sale now in progress.

~

Business does not come back. People must go after it.

~

A business genius is a man who knows the difference between being let in on a deal and being taken in on one.

~

A big shot is frequently an individual of small caliber and immense bore.

~

The difference between education and intelligence is that intelligence will make you a living.

~

Many Americans have energy crises on Mondays.

~

The work you put into your hours count more than the hours you put into your work.

~

If some folks practiced what they preached, they'd be working themselves to death.

~

It is estimated that the average man has two million brain cells, and most of them unemployed.

~

I think folks are foolish to put off until tomorrow what they can do today. If they like doing it today, they can do it again tomorrow.

~

Too many people are working themselves to death these days so they can live better.

~

The service station mechanic says, "It's a dirty business but we clean you good."

~

Many farmers are solving their farming problems by moving to the cities.

~

It is better to pull your own weight than to throw it around.

~

There are some workers who don't think. There are some thinkers who don't work.

~

Find a job or a business that you like and you'll never have to work during your lifetime.

~

For many years, a mining company out west employed a Chinese cook. One evening, after an unusually good dinner, the superintendent decided to raise his wages. The next day was pay day and the Chinese noted the extra money in his envelope. "Why you pay me more?" he asked.

"Because," replied the superintendent, "you've been such a good cook for all these years."

The Chinese thought it over, then said, "You been cheating me a long time, eh?"

~

An American tourist visiting Cork, Ireland noticed a man dozing in the shade of a large tree. "Don't you have a job?" The man said no. "Well, why don't you get yourself one instead of lazing about like this?"

"What for?" asked the man.

"So you can earn money," said the American.

"Why should I want to do that?" asked the local.

"So you could improve your standard of living. Then you could start saving."

"For what?"

"Well, when you've saved enough, you could retire and then you'd be able to take it easy and relax."

∼

A new salesman was complaining to an old-timer, "Every place I go, it seems the prospective customers in-sult me."

"That's strange," said the old-timer. "I've been working this territory for over twenty-five years. I've had my handbag dumped on the curb, been ushered out of offices by security guards, had doors slammed in my face, and even punched in the nose once. But I've never been insulted."

∼

The employer gave his new employee a broom. "Your first job," he said, "will be to sweep out the office.

"But," the new employee protested, "I'm a college graduate!"

"Very well," replied the boss. "Hand me the broom and I'll show you how."

∼

A merchant's report said that this was a crazy business, and it helps to be a little crazy when you try to run a business like this. One thing we can always be sure of — our price is never right. We say we want a hundred dollars for something and the customer says, "I'll give you fifty." Then we chew the rag for about an hour and he convinces us we are too high and we convince him that he is too low, and we get seventy-five, providing we put on sixty dollars worth of new parts, paint it, deliver it, and trade in his old machine for forty. The good part about this business is that both the customer and we are so confused by the time we have made the deal that we both think we came out ahead and we never know the difference until the end of the year. The auditor comes around and wants to know why we didn't make any money, especially after we sold so much stuff. We tell him he is a capitalist and that there are lots of nice things in this world besides money. Then we tell him about how friends and nice customers can't be bought with money, and we finally soften him up so much he doesn't even charge us for making out the audit.

QUESTIONS

Why do many great men come from small towns? Is it because of ambition or gossip?

∼

How can the devil do so much business from such a poor location?

∼

How many hours is weather forecasting behind arthritis?

∼

Do mothers cry at their daughter's weddings because the daughter is not getting the best man?

∼

When my wife says, "I love the simple things in life," why does she look at me?

∼

At my age, do I need a burning permit to light the candles on my birthday cake?

∼

Do drunk drivers pay stiff fines?

∼

Should we put newspaper under our cuckoo clock?

∼

What do you feed Christmas seals?

∼

If you want a nice looking nose, must you pick it?

∼

What does a dog do that man steps into? Pants.

∼

What do you do for a cold? Sneeze?

∼

Has he had any training besides potty?

∼

Do spoiled kids become stinkers?

∼

If I were arrested for being a Christian, would there be enough evidence to convict me?

∼

Is jumping to conclusions an exercise?

∼

When was the state of confusion admitted to the union?

∼

Why do so many economists think they know more about money than the people who have it?

~

Do bees hum because they don't know the words?

~

How many wheels are there on a football coach?

~

Does a grape stomper get fired for sitting down on the job?

~

If you want to get ahead, should you raise cabbage?

~

Bob Hope signed up for "how many wars?"

~

Is there much difference between a fat chance and a slim chance?

~

Is it free speech or is it cheap talk?

~

Why does God's work cost so much when the devil does it for nothing?

~

Do cows in a pasture say grace before they eat?

~

Did you roll with the punch on New Year's Eve?

~

How do those political jokes ever get elected?

~

Why do we drive on the parkway and park on the driveway?

~

Would an Indian chief call his wife "sweet Sioux?"

~

Is a flying saucer a dish that's out of this world?

~

Do the most promising politicians make the most promises?

~

When a politician promises a chicken in every pot, is that a birdbrain idea?

~

With the great strides we have made in transportation, is there such a thing as distant relatives anymore?

≈

If you must raise money to obtain a divorce, do you apply for a home improvement loan?

≈

Do you get pineapples from pine trees?

≈

Were Adam and Eve expelled from the Garden of Eden because they raised Cain?

≈

Are Eskimos God's frozen people?

≈

What do you give an elephant with diarrhea besides plenty of room?

≈

The meek shall inherit the earth. Does that include the mineral rights?

≈

Is modern art imagination without skill?

≈

When you become wrinkled with care and worry, is it time to have your faith lifted?

≈

I have a friend who is prospecting for oil. Is it appropriate to mail him a get well card?

≈

Why do people go fishing? For the halibut?

≈

Is installing an auto muffler exhausting work?

≈

Does your end justify your jeans?

≈

Have you seen a horse fly?

Have you seen a man eating chicken?

≈

Have you found a chicken dinner at the feed store?

≈

Is an English major a British officer?

≈

Do weathermen have their heads in the clouds?

~

Do you file your income tax or do you chisel on it?

~

Do you belong to the silent majority after marriage?

~

Do you argue with your doctor even though he has all the inside information?

~

What's the big deal about George Washington throwing a dollar across the Potomac? Doesn't Congress throw millions of dollars over the ocean every day?

~

When politicians air their differences, does that make them windbags?

~

If we elect a matador as president of the United States, would he be qualified to deal with all the bull from Congress?

~

If you were to eat some uranium, would you get atomic ache?

~

Often there is not enough time to do it right, but always enough time to do it over. Why?

~

Why don't all lawyers work together in an effort to stop truth decay?

~

Was Cain more able than his brother?

~

Does that guy remind you of a toothache you once had?

~

Will medical science ever find a cure for foot-in-mouth disease?

~

Why do we go to sleep when we're not sleepy and get up when we are sleepy?

~

How did Abraham Lincoln ever get an education without playing basketball?

~

If exercise is so good for us, why do so many athletes retire by age thirty-five?

∼

When babies are brought by the stork, are they the ones who grow up to be for the birds?

∼

If I go to an acupuncturist, will I become holier-than-thou?

∼

Are plastic surgeons experts at saving face?

∼

Do plastic surgeons accept credit cards?

∼

If the right half of the brain controls the left side of your body, and the left half of the brain controls the right side of the body, does that mean that left-handed people are the only ones in their right minds?

∼

Why was the cannibal's child not allowed to join in games with the missionary's son? Because his mother didn't want him playing with his food.

∼

Does he have a clear conscience or just a lousy memory?

∼

If you cross poison ivy with a four-leaf clover, do you get a rash of good luck?

∼

With digital clocks, will we still be able to turn back the hands of time?

∼

Does a lamp manufacturer have a bright future?

∼

Do window installers take great panes to please their customers?

∼

When architects argue, is that constructive criticism?

∼

Is the bakery business a rising career?

∼

When bricklayers retire, do they throw in their trowel?

∼

Do shepherds sing the song, "I've got plenty of mutton?"

~

Are people who are dressed to kill hunters?

~

If dogs are so dumb, how come they stay at home and sleep while their masters go to work?

~

If owls are so smart, why don't they get a day shift?

~

What's all this animal rights stuff? Do animals know their left from their right?

~

Do some people paint the town red because it matches the color of their eyes?

~

If you can't pay your bill at a sidewalk cafe, do they throw you in?

~

Did you hear about the cannibal who would not eat the millionaire because he was trying to give up rich food?

~

Do some corporations have so many vice presidents because there is so much vice to contend with?

~

Why are people so concerned about cash flow problems? Is it because you get cash and it flows out?

~

Why do they call it price fixing when it usually breaks you?

~

If money does not grow on trees, why do so many people go out on a limb for it?

~

When you see the bride and groom leave the church, is that watching the tied go out?

~

How many Americans with jobs are not working?

~

Why is it that whenever a witness offers to tell the truth, some lawyer objects?

~

Does that fellow have both feet planted firmly on the ground or does he normally move that slow?

∽

Why can't life's big problems come when we are eighteen and know everything?

∽

I found a dried leaf in an old Bible. Do you suppose it belongs to Adam or Eve?

∽

Who is worse off — a giraffe with a sore throat or a hippopotamus with chapped lips?

∽

When you jump from an airplane and the parachute doesn't open, is that jumping to a conclusion?

∽

Was Joan of Arc Noah's wife?

∽

What steps would you take if someone would come at you with a large, sharp knife? Big steps?

∽

If you learn to obey, does that prepare you to command?

∽

An old Roman prison has been unearthed. They found petrified remains of the prisoners. Were those hardened criminals?

∽

Is there such a thing as an idle rumor?

∽

Spinach is good for growing children. But who wants to grow children?

∽

Do grass widows get hay fever?

∽

Why is it that opportunity always knocks, but temptation walks right in?

∽

Spinster: "I have a dog that growls, a parrot that swears, a fireplace that smokes and a cat that stays out all night. Do I really need a husband?"

∽

A gerontologist explaining the facts about aging: "Your body replaces millions of cells every day." Old Timer: "How come my new cells are just as wrinkled as the old ones?"

◞

In Phoenix, the winters are so beautiful that heaven doesn't interest many people and the summers are so hot that hell doesn't scare them. Is this frustrating for a minister?

◞

We came into this world without riches and we will take no riches with us when we leave. Does that mean the stockbrokers are doing the Lord's work?

◞

Is it possible to be poor and happy at the same time?

◞

If nothing sticks to Teflon, how do they make Teflon stick to the pan?

◞

Why are there interstate highways in Hawaii?

◞

Why is it when you transport something by car it is called a shipment, but when you transport something by ship it is called cargo?

◞

If it weren't for doctors' offices, where would we put all those old magazines?

◞

Does the key to success fit your ignition?

◞

Do people who create the problems know the solutions?

◞

Is man's biggest problem outer space or is it too much inner space?

◞

Did you stop trying because you failed, or did you fail because you stopped trying?

◞

Test question: "What kind of a world would this be if everybody were just like me?"

◞

When girls throw themselves at men, is that called pitching curves?

◞

When you expect, do you deserve?

◞

Do men read *Playboy* for the same reason they read *National Geographic?* To see things they would otherwise not get a chance to see?

~

A five-year-old boy was asked, "With seven brothers and sisters, doesn't that cost a lot of money?" Little boy: "No, we don't buy them, we raise them."

~

How do caterpillars turn into butterflies?

~

How does a lady turn into a drugstore?

~

If you have words with your wife, is it best if you don't use yours?

~

When you are pushing eighty, is that enough exercise?

~

Are you a success when after seventy-seven years, you've had enough to eat and have escaped being eaten?

~

Why do old people who can no longer set bad examples like to give good advice?

~

When fortunetellers want to read your face, is that an indication that you're getting old?

~

How long do some graduates with a BA and an MA still depend on their PA and MA?

~

Why was the congresswoman alienated when the news media reported that her seat was up for grabs?

~

When you file your income tax, is it better to pay or deceive? Remember, it's all theirs.

~

Is income tax the fine you have to pay for thriving so fast?

~

Ted: "How does an eighty-year-old man like you get a gorgeous twenty-five-year-old bride?"
Harry: "I told her I was ninety-five."

~

I understand that the First National Bank Corporation now has banks all over hell. Does that mean we can now take it with us?

~

They claim you can catch more flies with honey than you can with vinegar. But who wants a lot of flies?

~

After falling down a flight of steps, a friend asked, "Did you miss a step?" "No, I hit every one of them."

~

How can you lose your life savings on something called securities?

~

Teacher: "What did Paul Revere say at the end of his famous ride?"
Pupil: "Whoa."

~

Not all these jokes are that old, are they? Dolly Parton was still wearing her training bra when they first came out.

~

If there are two sides to every question, why is there only one answer?

~

Wouldn't it be nice if we could sell our mistakes for what they cost us?

~

If it is such a small world, why are phone bills so high?

~

Why do women ask so many questions if their intuition is so good?

~

Is hell heaven's junkyard?

~

How does a loafer observe a holiday?

~

What happened to the money we were going to save by not smoking?

~

If people weren't meant to have a midnight snack, why do they put a light in the refrigerator?

DEFINITIONS

Ability: A talent for deciding something quickly and getting someone else to do it.

Acute: Pretty.

Adult Education: Started in a household with teenage children.

Adversity: The perfect diet to reduce a fat head.

Advice: Generally given by the bushel and taken by the grain.

Affirmation Specialist: A yes man.

Air Traffic Controller: One who has friends in high places.

Alarm Clock: A device designed to wake up people who don't have children.

Alimony: (a) War surplus; (b) Similar to paying installments on a car after you've wrecked it.

Ambition: Can get you into a lot of work.

Amiss: A young girl.

Antique Shop: Where you buy things that your grandparents threw away.

Apparent: A father or mother.

Ardor: An opening to a building.

Artery: The study of paintings.

Atheist's Club: A nonprophet organization.

Automatic Teller: The town gossip.

Average Man: One who thinks he isn't.

Bachelor: One who is footloose and fiancée free.

Balanced Diet: A diet soda and a candy bar — they cancel each other out.

Balanced Person: One who talks out of both sides of his mouth.

Bar Hopping: Saloon for rabbits.

Barium: What you have to do if you don't know CPR.

Big Bad John: A two-story outhouse.

Bigamist: (a) One who loves not wisely but too well; (b) A fellow who has one too many.

Bigotry: Being certain of something you know nothing about.

Bikini: Something that covers the overhead of a garment factory.

Biplane: The last word a pilot says before bailing out.

Born Executive: One whose father owns the business.

Brainstorm: An idea that is all wet.

Brat: A child that acts like your own but belongs to your neighbor.

Bridal Path: A church aisle.

Broker: Being poorer than you were previously.

Buccaneer: Too much to pay for corn.

Budget: A record of what the money should have been spent for.

Bullet: A small bull.

Caliber: The size of a bore.

Can Opener: A key to the bathroom.

Capitol Punishment: A new tax out of Washington.

Catalytic Converter: A missionary from Rome.

Census Taker: A person who goes from house to house increasing the population.

Character: The noblest of all possessions. Character is a victory, not a gift.

Cigarette: Used to draw your own conclusion.

Cigarette Girl: Cute vending machine.

Cigarettes: Killers that travel in packs.

Cloverleaf: California's state flower.

Coincide: What you do when it's raining.

Colic: A sheep dog.

Collectors' Items: Unpaid bills.

Collision: Two things coming together, like twins.

Coma: A punctuation mark.

Conference: A high-falutin' name for a coffee break.

Confidence: The ability to be wrong with absolute conviction.

Conscience: Something that can feel terrible when everything else feels swell.

Consequence: What you may get while results are what you want.

Contented: Having all the things your neighbor has.

Contentment: When your earning power equals your yearning power.

Convalescent: A patient who is still alive.

Count Down: A duck farmer taking inventory.

Courage: (a) The conquest of fear, not the absence of it; (b) When you're the only one who knows you're scared to death.

Courtship: The time period during which a girl tries to decide whether or not she can do better.

Coward: One who rides his bike on a high wire because he is afraid of traffic.

Curiosity: Freewheeling intelligence.

Cynic: A fellow who looks both ways before crossing a one-way street.

Defeat: What you walk with.

Defense: What keeps the cows at home.

Deficit: What you have when you haven't as much as you had when you had nothing.

Dental Office: Filling station.

Detail: Last thing over the fence.

Diet: Never eat while your wife is talking.

Dieting: Waiting for your hips to come in.

Dilate: Live longer.

Diplomacy: The ability to yawn without opening your mouth.

Diplomat: (a) One who remembers a lady's birthday but forgets her age; (b) One who can keep his shirt on while getting something off his chest.

Divorce: (a) When you would rather switch than fight; (b) Proves whose mother was right in the first place.

Doughnut: A person crazy about money.

Dream House: A house that costs twice as much as you dreamed it could.

Dry Dock: A thirsty physician.

Duty: That which you hate to do but love to brag about.

Economics: When your outgo exceeds your income, your upkeep will be your downfall.

Education: What you get from reading the fine print.

Egotism: Glue with which you get yourself stuck on.

Egotist: Someone never in doubt, but often in error.

Einstein: One beer.

Energy: Something your children save for a rainy day.

English Channel: A British TV station.

Entitlement Program: Money we give to the government, less handling charges, which is given back to the people.

Europe: A collection of countries with chips on their shoulders and none on the table.

Evolution: Why so many parents go ape over their kids' behavior.

Expectant Father: Man studying for the priesthood.

Experience: (a) What you get from not reading the fine print; (b) The sum total of all the things you really didn't want to know in the first place; (c) Something you get when you're looking for something else; (d) Compulsory education.

Extravagance: The foolish spending habits of someone else.

Facts: Constitute a great force in the world when combined with good ideas.

Fame: Something the famous are usually too dead to enjoy.

Family Man: One who replaces the money in his wallet with snapshots.

Family Reunion: Nest of kin.

Fashion: Something that goes out of style as soon as everybody has one.

Fast: What you do while you try to get the waiter's attention.

Fathers: People who give away their daughters to men who aren't nearly good enough so they can have grandchildren who are smarter than all the other kids.

Fester: (a) Quicker; (b) To go at a higher speed.

Fetter: What you get when you eat too much.

Fetus: What some relatives do when we visit them.

Figure of Speech: Talk about dieting.

Filibuster: When a senator talks a long time without saying anything.

Filing Cabinet: A place to lose things alphabetically.

Flattery: What makes husbands out of bachelors.

Flood: When a river gets too big for its bridges.

Floodlights: What Noah used to illuminate his ark.

Fly Ball: A dance for bugs.

Flying Saucer: A dish that's out of this world.

Forbidden Fruit: Responsible for bad jam.

Ford Foundation: A new kind of girdle.

Free Speech: What teenagers get from their parents.

Friend: A friend is a person with whom you can be yourself.

Frustration: Wife who finds a letter she gave to her husband to mail three months ago in the coat that has been at home waiting for a button to be sewed on.

Future: The time when folks will be wishing they'd done all the things they aren't doing now.

Garage Sale: Where money changes hands and objects are moved from one garage to another.

Gigolo: A guy who earns his living by the sweat of his Frau.

Girdle: A device to keep an unfortunate situation from spreading.

Glamour Girl: One who has what it takes to take what you have.

Gold Digger: (a) A girl with a gift of grab; (b) A girl that breaks dates by going out with them; (c) A girl who will date any man that can pass the asset test.

Golf: A lot of walking broken up by disappointments and bad arithmetic.

Good Conversationalist: One who shares your opinion.

Gossip: (a) Mouth-to-mouth recitation; (b) Something negative that is developed and then enlarged.

Grace: When you can put your best foot forward without stepping on any toes.

Grit: Something that lies on the bottom of a birdcage.

Hamlet: A little pig.

Hangover: The wrath of grapes.

Happiness: (a) The state of being too busy to be miserable; (b) A healthy mental attitude, a grateful spirit, a clear conscience and a heart full of love.

Hick Town: Where there's no good place to do wrong.

Hillbilly: Mountain goat.

Homesickness: What you feel about ten minutes after you sign the mortgage note.

Hometown: Where people wonder how you ever made it as far as you did.

Honesty: A word now preceded by "old-fashioned."

Hope: A precious gift. Without hope, all appears lost. With hope, there is a glimmer of light in the worst situation.

Horn of Plenty: The sound of a traffic jam.

House Broke: What you are after building a new house.

Humility: (a) The sense you experience when you check yourself in a clothing store's three-way mirror; (b) The ability to attract attention while looking modest.

Illegal: A sick bird.

Inflation: (a) A state of affairs in which you never had so much money nor parted with it so fast; (b) The art of cutting a dollar into many parts without touching the paper.

Inheritance: A popular labor-saving device.

Insistence: When persistence meets resistance.

Install: Where you put cows while you milk them.

Intent: Where campers go when it rains.

International Date Line: What are you doing tonight, toots?

Intuition: What tells a wife that her husband has done something wrong before he even thinks of doing it.

Irony: When all your life you've saved for a rainy day, then get transferred to Nevada.

IRS: Income Removal Service.

Jailbirds: Birds found in captivity.

Jeep: The nearest thing to a mechanical mule.

Johnny Cash: A pay toilet.

Jury: Twelve people chosen to decide who has the best lawyer.

Juvenile Delinquent: A youngster who has been given a free hand but not in the proper place.

Keep Right: The world's shortest sermon.

Kentucky Derby: A hat.

Kindness: The ability to love people more than they really deserve.

Labor Saving Device: Money.

Lame Duck: A politician whose goose has been cooked.

Last Resort: What you're stuck with when you make your vacation plans late.

Laugh: A smile with a soundtrack.

Laughter: The shortest distance between two people.

Leadership: Action, not position.

Lenten Menu: Fast food.

Liberty: A hard-won achievement with the help of God.

Liquid Assets: Inventory of your liquor.

Liquor: A liquid that makes a man tight and his tongue loose.

Love: (a) When you know you were made for each other; marriage is when you start making alterations; (b) Something that makes you feel funny and act foolish.

LSD: Love, security and discipline.

Luck: When preparation meets opportunity.

Lunatic: Insect from the moon.

Manure: The other word the farmer's wife wants her husband to use.

Marriage: Like a cafeteria. You pick out what looks good to you and pay for it down the line.

Membrane: The part of your brain you remember with.

Menu: Consumer's guide.

Mid-life Crisis: Too tired to work and too broke to quit.

Middle Age: When your memory is shorter, your experience longer, your stamina lower and your forehead higher.

Minister: Travel agent for outer space.

Minor Operation: An operation on someone else.

Mischief: The chief's daughter.

Misjudge: A lady judge who is not married.

Mixed Emotions: Seeing your mother-in-law go over the cliff in your brand new Lincoln.

Model Child: These days, a child without a police record.

Monastery: Home for unwed fathers.

Money: A good laborsaving device.

Mortgage Broker: Loan arranger.

Mushroom: A room to hold hands.

Natural Death: When you die by yourself without the help of a doctor.

Necessities: Food, clothing, shelter, credit cards and any luxury you see in your neighbor's home.

New Parents: People who have their ups and downs in the middle of the night.

Nitrates: Cheaper than day rates.

Nose Pollution: The common cold.

Nothing: Something some people are good for.

Obesity: Surplus gone to waist.

Obstetrician: Delivery boy.

Oil Drilling: A boring profession.

Old Age: Unplanned obsolescence.

Open Mind: Holes in one's head.

Opportunist: (a) Someone who becomes a veterinarian when the world goes to the dogs; (b) A person who goes ahead and does what you always intended to do.

Optimist: (a) A fisherman who takes along a camera; (b) Someone who thinks he can live like a millionaire if he has a million dollars; (c) A person who grabs a fishing pole when he discovers his basement is flooded; (d) A person who thinks that a housefly is looking for a way out.

Oral Surgery: Cutting your speech in half.

Orthopedist: One who gets the breaks.

Overdressed: When a person is all wrapped up in himself.

Pants: What a dog does.

Paradox: Two doctors.

Parasite: Two building lots.

Paratrooper: A soldier who climbs down from trees he never climbed up.

Parenting: On-the-job training.

Parents: Father Time and Mother Nature.

Patience: A minor form of despair portrayed as a virtue.

Pediatrician: A person with little patients.

People of Stature: People who don't need status.

Perfect Man: The one your wife claims she should have married.

Period Furniture: An electric chair because it ends a sentence.

Perpetual Youth: To lie about your age.

Persistence: The forerunner of success, the father of victory, the ancestor of accomplishments.

Pessimist: One who has financed too many optimists.

Pesto: A bother to an Italian chef.

Petty Larceny: Stealing a kiss.

Phone Booth: Chatter box.

Poise: (a) The ability to be ill at ease inconspicuously; (b) The art of raising an eyebrow instead of the roof.

Police Helicopter: The whirlybird that catches the worm.

Politics: The art of obtaining money from the rich and votes from the poor on the pretext of protecting the two from each other.

Popover: What happens when you put too many kernels in the corn popper.

Potty Training: A trickle down theory.

Practical Nurse: One who marries a millionaire.

Prejudice: Being down on something you're not up on.

Prenuptial Agreement: Usually an agreement drafted by an attorney to protect the party of the first part from the party of the second part and to protect the party of the second part from the party of the first part in the event the party is over. This agreement covers seven pages, which the attorney calls a brief.

Procrastination: Fertilizer that makes difficulties grow and the grave where opportunity is buried.

Profanity: (a) A short cut to thinking; (b) The use of strong words by weak people.

Professor: One who goes to college and never gets out.

Progress: Now, paying out much more in taxes than we formerly received in wages.

Pun: Humor that causes everyone to groan and is meant to punish the hearers.

Puppy Love: Beginning of a dog's life.

Quack: A doctor who ducks the law.

Quadruplets: Four crying out loud.

Quaint House: Run down.

Race Difficulties: Picking the wrong horse.

Racehorse: An animal that can take several thousand people for a ride at the same time.

Raving Beauty: One who came in last in a beauty contest.

Realtor: A person who is always putting someone in their place.

Recession: A time when we have to do without a lot of things our grandparents never heard of.

Refrigerator: A place to store leftovers until they're ready to be thrown out.

Religious Freedom: To some, the choice of churches they may stay away from.

Reno: A large inland seaport in the United States with the tide running in and the untied running out.

Report Card: A piece of paper that makes you realize you don't have to be a weight lifter to raise a dumbbell.

Resort: A place where people go for change and the landlord gets the rest.

Retirement: (a) When you're not dead yet, but you have many of the symptoms; (b) Twice as much spouse on half as much money.

Rhubarb: Bloodshot celery.

Royal Flush: When kings get embarrassed.

Saloon Arthritis: One who gets stiff in a different joint every night has this ailment.

Sanitary Belt: Booze from a clean shot glass.

Service: The rent we pay for the space we occupy in the world.

Sex: Something you use to carry your potatoes in — comes in burlap, plastic or paper.

Skunk: A cat with fluid drive.

Small Town: Where everyone knows whose credit is good and whose children are not.

Smile: A curve that sets many things straight.

Smiles: The longest word. There's a mile between the first and last letter.

Smirk: A smile that doesn't work.

Snorer: The one who falls asleep first.

Social Grace: When you start out on the right foot instead of putting it in your mouth.

Socialized Medicine: Women meeting and talking about their operations.

Spare Ribs: What man used to have before God created woman.

Sponge Cake: When you sponge the ingredients from your neighbors to bake the cake.

St. Louis Cardinals: Are appointed by the Pope.

Stalemate: A spouse who is beginning to smell.

Stern Punishment: A spanking.

Strapless Gown: When a woman won't shoulder the responsibility.

Striptease Dancer: A girl who never puts off until tomorrow what she can put off today.

Success: A series of failures held together by the strong strands of determination and persistence.

Suspended Sentence: He will hang.

Suspenders: Social security.

Sweater: A garment worn by children when the mother feels chilly.

Tact: The ability to close your mouth before somebody else does.

Taxpayer: Political prisoner.

Television: Called a medium because it is not rare or well done.

Tenderfoot: A person who, after riding a horse all day, finds it's not his feet that are tender.

Thief: A person who has the habit of finding things before the owner loses them.

Three Collective Nouns: (a) flypaper; (b) wastebasket; (c) vacuum cleaner.

Tolerance: The positive and cordial effort to understand another's beliefs, practices and habits without necessarily sharing or accepting them.

Topless Bar: A pub without a roof.

Totalitarian State: A place where the people in jail are better than the people who put them there.

Toy Poodle: A poodle that runs on batteries.

Translator: A person who gives lip service.

Tree Surgeon: Branch manager.

Triumph: The "umph" added to try.

Tulips: The standard number of lips assigned to each person.

Unaware: The last thing you take off at night.

Undercover Agent: Saleslady in the lingerie department.

Underprivileged: (a) Today's teenager who has to play his guitar without electricity; (b) Not having a remote control for your color television set.

User Friendly: Someone who shakes your hand before election and your confidence after election.

Vacation: Two weeks that are too short, after which you are too tired to go home and too broke not to.

Vanguard: A person who protects trucks.

Varicose Veins: Veins very close together.

Video Aerobics: Getting up and down from your recliner to change tapes.

Virg and Mary: The parents of Jesus.

Waiter: Someone who believes money grows on trays.

Wedding Band: A one-man band.

Weight Watcher: A man who waits and watches while his wife is shopping.

Wife: A lie detector without wires.

Work: (a) An unpopular way of earning money; (b) The annoyance people have to endure between coffee breaks; (c) Medication for a good night's sleep.

Worry: Interest paid on trouble before it falls due.

Youthful Figure: What you get when you ask a woman her age.

Zoo: A place of refuge where wild animals are protected from people.

THE OUTHOUSE
CONTRIBUTIONS FROM FRIENDS

Last Will of Mr. Farmer

I Leave:

To my wife, my overdraft at the bank — maybe she can explain it.

To my banker, my soul — he has the mortgage on it anyway.

To my neighbor, my clown suit — he'll need it if he continues to farm as he has in the past.

To the ASCS, my grain bin — I was planning to let them take it next year anyway.

To the county agent, 50 bushels of corn to see if he can hit the market — I never could.

To the junk man, all my machinery — he's had his eye on it for years.

To my undertaker, a special request — I want six implement and fertilizer dealers for my pallbearers. They are used to carrying me.

To the weatherman, rain and sleet and snow for the funeral — no sense in having good weather now.

To the gravedigger — don't bother. The hole I'm in now should be big enough.

~

Come to Rochester, Minnesota

HAVING TAKEN A "FEW TOO MANY" AT A LOCAL BAR, A PRETTY young girl ran outdoors, fainted and fell over a trash barrel. A young man saw her, picked her up and carried her to his car. The next morning he wired his partner in Chicago: "Close office ... Sell everything ... Come to Rochester. They throw away better stuff than you can buy in Chicago."

~

The Joys of Aging

I HAVE BECOME QUITE A FRIVOLOUS OLD GAL. I'M SEEING FIVE gentlemen every day. As soon as I awake, Will Power helps me out of bed. When he leaves, I go see John. Then Charlie Horse comes along, and when he is here he takes a lot of my attention. When he leaves, Arthur Ritis shows up and stays the rest of the day. He doesn't like to stay in one place very long, so he takes me from joint to joint. After such a busy day I'm really tired and ready to go to bed with Ben Gay. What a day!

~

An Irish Prayer

MAY THOSE THAT LOVE US, LOVE US; AND THOSE THAT DON'T LOVE us, may God turn their hearts; and if He doesn't turn their hearts, may He turn their ankles so we'll know them by their limping.

~

A NICE LADY FROM ARIZONA WAS PLANNING A WEEK'S VACATION IN the north woods. Before confirming her reservation, she wanted to make sure that the campground had adequate facilities. Uppermost in her mind were toilet facilities, but she couldn't bring herself to write "toilet" in her letter. After considerable deliberation, she settled on "bathroom commode," but when she wrote the letter, she thought it still sounded too forward. So when she wrote to the campground, she referred to the bathroom commode as B.C. "Does the campground have its own B.C.?" is what she actually wrote.

Well, the campground owner was a bit puzzled about the request, so he showed the letter around to several other campers, but they couldn't decipher it either. Finally the campground owner figured that she must be referring to the location of a Baptist Church in the area and wrote back:

Dear Madam:

I take pleasure in informing you that a B.C. is located just a few miles from our campground and is capable of seating 250 people at one time. I admit that it is quite a distance if you are in the habit of going regularly, but no doubt you will be pleased to know that a great number of people take their lunches along and make a day of it. They usually arrive early and stay late. The last time my wife and I went was six years ago and it was so crowded we had to stand up the whole time we were there. Right now a supper is planned to raise money to buy more seats. They are going to hold it in the basement of the B.C. I would like to say it pains me very much not to be able to go more regularly, but it is surely no lack of desire on my part. As we grow older, it seems to be more of an effort, particularly in cold weather. If you do decide to come to our campground, perhaps I could go with you the first time and sit with you and introduce you to all the other folks.

Hope to see you soon,

John Henry, Owner

≈

Donkey Racing in Texas

A PREACHER WANTED TO RAISE MONEY FOR HIS CHURCH, AND BEING told there was a fortune in horse racing, he decided to purchase one and enter him in the races. However, at the local auction, the going price for horses was so steep, the preacher ended up buying a donkey instead.

He figured that since he had it, he might as well go ahead and enter it in the races. To his surprise, the donkey came in third. The next day the racing form carried this headline: "PREACHER'S ASS SHOWS."

The preacher was so pleased with the donkey that he entered it in the races again. This time he won. The next day the racing form read: "PREACHER'S ASS OUT IN FRONT." The Bishop was so upset with this kind of publicity he ordered the preacher not to enter the donkey in another race. The headline that day read: "BISHOP SCRATCHES PREACHER'S ASS."

This was too much for the Bishop and he ordered the preacher to get rid of the animal. The preacher decided to give the donkey to Lena. The headline the next day read: "LENA HAS BEST ASS IN TOWN." The preacher fainted.

He informed Lena that she would have to dispose of the donkey. She finally found a farmer who was willing to buy the animal for ten dollars. The next day the paper stated, "LENA PEDDLES ASS FOR TEN BUCKS." They buried the Bishop the next day.

∾

A Child's View of Retirement in a Mobile Home Park

AFTER SPRING BREAK, THE TEACHER ASKED HER THIRD GRADE CLASS to write a composition on their holiday. One little boy wrote as follows:

We always spend Easter with Grandma and Grandpa. They used to live here in a big brick house, but Grandpa got retarded and they moved to Florida. They live in a place with a lot of other retarded people. They live in little tin huts. They ride big three-wheel bicycles. They go to a building they call the wrecked room, but it's fixed now. They play games there and do exercises, but not very well. There is a swimming pool, and they go into it and just stand there with their hats on. I guess they don't know how to swim. My Grandma used to bake cookies and stuff, but I guess she forgot how. They all go to restaurants that are fast. Nobody cooks anymore. As you go into their park, there is a dollhouse with a man sitting in it. He watches them all so they can't get out without him seeing them. They wear badges with their names on them. I guess they don't know who they are.

My Grandma says that Grandpa worked hard all of his life and earned his retardment. I wish they would move back home, but I guess the man in the dollhouse won't let them out.

≈

Notice

THIS COMPANY REQUIRES NO PHYSICAL FITNESS PROGRAM. Everyone here gets enough exercise jumping to conclusions, flying off the handle, carrying things too far, dodging responsibilities and pushing their luck.

Freedom Isn't Free

I watched the flag pass by one day
It fluttered in the breeze.
A young marine saluted it.
And then he stood at ease.

I looked at him in uniform,
So young, so tall, so proud;
With hair cut square and eyes alert,
He'd stand out in any crowd.

I thought how many men like him
Had fallen through the years.
How many died on foreign soil?
How many mothers' tears?

How many pilots' planes shot down?
How many died at sea?
How many foxholes were soldiers' graves?
No, freedom is not free.

I heard the sound of taps one night
When everything was still.
I listened to the bugler play,
And felt a sudden chill.

I wondered just how many times
That taps had meant "amen."
When a flag had covered a coffin
Of a brother or a friend.

I thought of all the children,
Of the mothers and the wives,
Of fathers' sons, and husbands,
With interrupted lives.

I thought about a graveyard
At the bottom of the sea,
Of unmarked graves in Arlington.
No, freedom is not free.

ROTC CADET, MAJOR KELLY STRONG
HOMESTEAD SENIOR HIGH SCHOOL

Order Information

Order *Horse Sense For Stable Minds* from your bookstore.

If unavailable at your bookstore, please send $24.95 plus $2.50 for shipping and handling. Add $.50 for each additional book. Quantity discounts are available. Please contact the publisher.

Michigan residents please add 6% sales tax.

Send _____ book(s).

PLEASE PRINT

Name: _____

Address: _____

_____

City:_____

State: _____ Zip: _____

Telephone: _____

Send check or money order (payable to *Sage Creek Press*) plus above information to:

Sage Creek Press
121 E. Front Street, 4th Floor
Traverse City, MI 49684
(616) 933-0445

Erwin G. Walth
121 14th St NE, Suite 801
Rochester, MN 55906
(507) 285-0297